Economics of
Petroleum Market

By

Roshdy Ebrahim, Ph.D

Copyright © 2018 Roshdy Ebrahim

All right reserved

ISBN: 9781980781363

Preface

The year 1857 marked the beginning of commercial petroleum production in Rumania, followed in 1859 by the discovery of oil in Pennsylvania. Petroleum was found by the drillers under "Colonel" Drake, and crude refineries were soon built to separate the fractions. The most important fraction was kerosene, known as "illuminating oil", which rapidly became the dominant global fuel for lamps (replacing whale oil). In the early days, refinery output was about 50% kerosene, 10% gasoline, 10% lubricating oil, 10–15% fuel oil and the rest consisting of losses and miscellaneous by-products like tar.

Natural gas is currently the number three fossil fuel in terms of share of the global primary energy mix and for years the world has debated the potential for natural gas to play a critical part in building a more resilient and sustainable energy future. While the demand outlook is currently uncertain, advances in supply side technologies for unconventional resource development, led by advances in US shale gas operations, have changed the supply landscape and created new prospects for affordable and secure supplies of natural gas.

With the influx of added supplies outpacing demand growth, the world is faced with a global supply glut and depressed natural gas prices, and suppliers with large inflexible investments in natural gas assets are scrambling to stay afloat. More than one year into a down market, the resilience of unconventional gas, such as shale gas and coal bed methane (CBM), continues to reshape the international energy supply landscape. Just a few years ago, unconventional gas was considered a high-cost asset that required $100 per barrel (bbl) oil to survive. However, in North America, operational efficiencies and technology innovation drove cost reductions, improved productivity, and enabled an unconventional gas supply revolution more quickly than many policymakers and industry stakeholders could have imagine.

Continued demand for oil- and gas-based energy services throughout the twenty first century is expected to induce technological change that could lower future production cost levels. On the other hand, environmental considerations could adversely affect oil and gas production costs, especially when unconventional resources are considered. Production of these resources typically has larger environmental impacts, including increased greenhouse gases emitted during the extraction and upgrading processes. Emissions penalties could change the shapes of the supply curves, as unconventional oil and gas would become relatively more expensive.

The approach for developing the supply cost curves in this study is based on and begins by using European conventional oil and gas volumes estimated by the Variable Shape Distribution (VSD) model. The volumes are distributed into several classes based on resource quality. Every class is then assigned lower and upper bounds of production costs, resulting in supply cost curves. The unconventional oil and gas quantities are taken from the Global Energy Assessment, while the associated production costs are based on IEA. For both oil and gas, two curves are developed—one assumes current technology and the other technology performance for 2030.

However, the problems we face as global oil supply becomes increasingly difficult are somewhat different. This is because, first, oil can be substituted by other forms of energy in almost any activity. Aero planes, for example, can fly on biofuels or liquid hydrogen; trucks be run on compressed natural gas; cars on gas or electricity; houses and offices be heated and cooled by electricity or by other fuels; and industrial chemicals produced from gas, coal or biomass, or directly from solar energy using ubiquitous feedstocks. Second, given sufficient warning, society can choose to change its activities and priorities so as to use less oil.

Contents

Preface 3

Contents 6

Introduction 8

1. Energy and oil Prices 13
   1.1. WORLD ENERGY POLICY 41
   1.2. Energy Demand 46
   1.3. The Elasticity of Demand 48
   1.4. Energy Efficiency 48
   1.5. World Economy and Energy Consumption Are Significantly Correlated . 54
   1.6. The Economic Drivers of the Political Will for Social Responsibility in Energy Policy for Fossil Fuel Exporting Countries 59
   1.7. Crude Oil Pricing 62
   1.8. OIL PRICE HISTORY 77
   1.9. FUTURE OF OIL 80
   1.10. How Prices Reacted to the Shale Revolution 81
2. Supply and demand 96
   2.1. Oil demand 103
   2.2. oil supply 125
   2.3. Natural gas demand 132
   2.4. Natural Gas supply 146

- 2.5. Oil and Gas Production Costs 156
  - 2.5.1. Supply Cost Curves 165
- 2.6. Petroleum Price Reforms in china. 174
- 3. Petroleum market 176
  - 3.1. WORLD SUPPLY STRUCTURE 176
    - 3.1.1. Structure of Oil Industry 179
    - 3.1.2. Structure of the Gas Industry 184
  - 3.2. Oil Marketing 188
  - 3.3. The Effect of the Relationship Between Oil Price and Stock Markets in Energy Sustainable Countries 191
  - 3.4. Global LNG Markets 194
  - 3.5. Oil and Gas Accounting 204
  - 3.6. The World Crude Oil Paradoxes 207
  - 3.7. Final market and export prices 218
  - 3.8. Revenue items 223
- References 225
- Biography of the author 230

Introduction

The pricing regimes of energy commodities have undergone several evolutions since oil and natural gas began being traded on a global scale. The mechanisms for setting prices are meant to reflect the value of those commodities based on supply and demand, and the overall value of that energy trade. In reality, while the trading prices reported by futures exchanges do reflect what the market believes those commodities are worth at a particular time, they do not accurately show the price of oil and gas being consumed throughout the world since there are numerous energy deals that are made outside of the scope of commodities exchanges, making it impossible to gage the value of the trade looking strictly at futures prices. Th e anomalies between exchange prices and prices charged domestically by energy producers or those charged by exporters vary because so many countries that are energy exporters have nationalized energy industries which allow the governments of those states to intervene in energy deals and often sell that energy at prices that are not connected to the trading price at exchanges. Th us, oil and natural gas are somewhat unique among the many commodities that are traded on exchanges with private companies often being the producers in countries with nationalized energy sectors, making it impossible to completely separate business from politics in oil and gas pricing. [1]

Oil is an important commodity in today's world, which influences the daily life of every individual, impacts the economic growth and development of every nation, and influences the world economy to such an extent that no other commodity can match. Oil pricing is a sensitive issue; therefore, it is important that oil price should be fair to both producers and consumers for sustainable growth and judicious consumption. we would discuss the importance, sensitivity, and complexities involved in oil pricing and would develop a linear programming (LP) model to optimize base oil price for a country.

Oil pricing is a complex issue and is not governed by economic criteria alone—a host of socio-political and other factors influence it. This study aims to optimize base oil price taking into account the cost and share of domestic oil production and that of imported oil, effect of reserves life on price, effect of substitute to oil, and so on. It develops an optimization model using LP method, which has the capability to study and measure the impact of varying parameters under different scenarios.

Formula prices define the official selling prices (OSPs) that crude oil exporters

---

[1]Thijs Van de Graaf • Benjamin K. Sovacool Arunabha Ghosh • Florian Kern • Michael T. Klare: The Palgrave Handbook of the International Political Economy of Energy. 2016. P 225

charge their customers on term contracts. They relate (via premiums or discounts) the sale price of an exported crude oil cargo to the spot or forward price of a reference or 'marker' crude. Mexico first adopted this method in early 1986 and Middle Eastern oil exporters widely accepted it soon after.

This change occurred in the aftermath of the 1985–86 collapse of the previous decade's administered pricing system, in which OPEC ministers set reference prices. The failure of the administered pricing system forced GCC OPEC countries to begin selling crude oil in a market-responsive manner. To avoid being price leaders, key GCC OPEC crude exporters had to compete with growing non-OPEC crude oil supplies in the 1980s and 1990s such that a two-tier pricing regime did not emerge, as it did under the administered price system.

In the aftermath of 1985–86, OPEC crude prices had to be market determined, not market determining. This could only be achieved by fixing a relationship with freely traded regional reference crude oils (such as West Texas Intermediate, Brent, and Dubai) with prices discovered in large, liquid markets. As remarked by H.E. Ali Al-Naimi, the Saudi Minister of Petroleum and Mineral Resources.

As most Middle East crude is sold on term contracts on a free-on-board (FOB) basis according to formula-based OSPs, there is little room to differentiate among suppliers, as each exporter's term contracts are fixed for all term contract customers in the region. At the margin, however, the NOC that is the first to announce the monthly OSPs (typically Saudi Aramco) faces one disadvantage: that other suppliers can then offer a slightly better discount when announcing their own monthly OSPs. [1]

Both buyer and seller clearly benefit from joint crude storage arrangements. The respective costs and benefits to the sellers and buyers of leased storage will be a function of the commercial terms of each deal, including the opportunity costs of storage tanks to their owner and how both buyer and seller optimize the use of their shipping fleets. Furthermore, for the buyer a joint oil storage deal also includes the social benefits of enhanced energy security, as measured by the increase in the host country's strategic petroleum reserves. For the seller, it might give the assurance that the buyer will face higher transaction costs in exiting the joint venture storage agreement and making alternative arrangements for maintaining a strategic petroleum reserve.

To that extent, the crude seller's perception of security of demand might be enhanced. But it is nevertheless clear that all

---

[1] Leo Lester: Energy Relations and Policy Making in Asia. 2016. P 65: 66

buyers of crude within a region face the same OSP charged by any particular Middle East NOC. If OSPs are too often 'out of the market', meaning overpriced, buyers will naturally re-assess the value of joint venture storage arrangements and, if necessary, turn to alternative sources of crude supplies and terminate such arrangements. [1]

---

[1]Leo Lester: Energy Relations and Policy Making in Asia. 2016. P 68

1. Energy and oil Prices

Energy security that fueled the creation of the international energy agency (IEA) in 1974 relates the concepts of national security and the availability of natural resources for energy consumption (between its member states).

Historically, the concept of energy security was primarily linked to securing oil supply. The availability or uninterrupted physical delivery at a price which is affordable, in the light of the 1973 oil crisis, was a key concern for modern and developing economies whose functioning was heavily dependent on. In the subsequent years, the rate of industrial and population growth of developing countries, as much as the excessive reliance of developed countries to energy supply, has given rise to the uneven distribution of energy supplied among countries. In response to the finite availability of energy sources, rising costs of extraction, and other energy security threats, recent literature of energy security aims to delineate its dimensions. van Vuuren et al. (2009) and a recent study of the US Chamber of Commerce (2010) represent (in an equivalent manner) energy security, at least in the longer term, as availability (geological), accessibility (geopolitical), affordability (economic), and acceptability (environmental and social). Further studies by Gupta (2008) emphasize the definition of energy security, at least in the short term, as the economic cost and physical availability. This definition comes in the sound of the IEA's definition, which in a recent study Jewell (2011) defines the factors of energy security at an international level to risk exposure and resilience, associated with potential disruptions of energy imports and the ability of energy systems to adapt to or withstand disruptions, respectively.

Policy makers often equate the attainment of energy security with energy independence, which looks at reducing country imports of foreign sources of energy. Each term length in energy security has the relevant implications. Longer term is mainly linked to timely investments to supply energy in line with economic developments and environmental needs. It also implies the requirement to address sustainable developments as alternatives to conventional technologies. On the other hand, short-term energy security is the ability of the energy system to react promptly to sudden changes in supply and demand that directly affect the price of the energy product. In addition, in Jaromir et al. (2012), it is argued that equating security with independence also leads policy makers to focus on expanding domestic supplies, rather than on efficient methods to manage risk by diversifying suppliers or diversifying fuel types.

Though alternative technologies may have a promising and prominent effect in the view towards a sustainable economic growth, world fossil fuel demand is likely to grow at least over the next decade and remain a significant part of the energy mix. Remaining reserves of the fundamental factors of energy production, gas and oil, are increasingly concentrated in a limited number of countries increasing the relationship of price and demand.

The United States official international oil policy during the 1980s and early 1990s was to ensure a smooth transfer of Middle East oil to support world market demand. The energy security at that stage aimed to ensure stability in oil prices. It is argued that the economic growth during the mid-1990s, especially in Asia, in relation to the increased demand for oil during that period, had similarities with the period of the early 1970s as noted in El-Gamal and Jaffe (2010). The large increase in oil prices over the 2007–2008 period did raise again the profile of energy security with relation to demand/supply imbalances. While energy security focus has many aspects, it is argued that the notional driving force to energy security, apart the finite resources that produce the worlds energy, is the price of oil. In the early 2011, even with domestic tax components being reduced, the prices of fuel in many countries reached top levels at the height of the Libya crisis. The primary driving force of oil prices now, compared to 2011, is the emerging market demand through the means of commodity intense nations. According to a statement at J.P. Morgan Asset Management, the risk is not how high prices are elevated, but the length of the period that prices will remain high. The effect of current oil price changes to equity markets is well documented in current literature. Arouri et al. (2012) examine the impact of oil price changes to the equity sector and, in particular, examine the necessity of making oil assets part of a well-diversified portfolio of sector stocks to effectively hedge the oil price risk. This comes into agreement with the established argument of a well-diversified portfolio of many different assets. Banks as a whole are typically very well diversified and aware of the benefits of diversification in their daily balances. The essence of energy security is again at focus of oil prices either through the means of diversifying the energy sources (in the longer-term horizon) or by creating a hedge portfolio to minimize the impact of price spikes (in the shorter-term horizon). Practically, short-lived price spikes are not the driving force that leads an economy into recession nor the cause of investors changing significantly their asset allocations. Looking at the oil price changes from mid-2011 to early 2012, we note that it took approximately 6 months for oil prices to return to their pre-distressed level.

Kilian (2009) distinguishes between three major drivers of oil price changes. He notes that aggregate demand for goods and precautionary demand for oil are the main drivers for oil price spikes and that disruptions in oil supply in the form of political instability or similar reasons are negligible in price changes. Contradictory Hamilton (2009) finds that temporarily physical oil supply disruptions had a major role in explaining historical dynamics of oil movements and argues that stagnating world oil production may also be accounted for the 2007–2008 oil price trending. The author argues that it is the short-run elasticities of substitutions between oil and other factors of production and notes that these elasticities get larger over longer horizons, as agents seek to diversify to oil substitutes. Further, it is essentially the argument that oil reserves are ultimately finite, and the fact that oil which is extracted easy and at lower cost is produced (and refined first), and cumulated amount of oil already produced, makes the process more expensive.

The future price of oil is notoriously difficult to predict. The studies of Alquist et al. (2011) find that oil price forecasts based on the monthly spreads of oil futures markets and with oil spot markets provide no better forecasts than random walk models. The conflicting results in the academic and practitioner literature are heavily biased by the definition of oil price forecasts. Alquist et al. (2011) further note that when it comes to describing oil price forecasts, there is not precise reference to whether the corresponding study emphasizes in prices of oil in real or nominal terms. Further, the estimation and evaluation period need to clarified.

The most common question in estimating parameters of the underlying model/ process has to do with the sample period used. While including longer periods one manages to capture the business cycle, estimation in shorter periods tend to reflect more accurately short-term price dynamics.

In the light of the above discussion, as many authors have realistically shown that even a multifactor model cannot predict oil price changes, we provide a comprehensive empirical analysis of oil price dynamics using documented and well-known (in the field of finance) continuous-time processes, rather than providing a framework that aims to forecast the future price of oil. Our focus lies on the management of risk perspective. As oil spikes can last from days to week, we note that it is not possible to determine the exact period that prices will change or stay elevated. In contrast, we provide the tools for modeling perspectives with respect to managing as accurately as possible oil price risk by looking at the underlying process distribution. Policy makers who seek to get an empirical view of price evolution in the short run or portfolio managers to aim to diversify their portfolios as best as possible may employ the process that suitably fits the current market dynamics. We partially examine whether the dynamics of the market are more suitably represented by a continuous-time process with complicated drift and volatility dynamics. We also investigate, in the light of the paper of Geman (2005), whether processes with mean-reverting drift to a long-run equilibrium can still provide a better fit.

For the estimation of the parameters of the underlying process, we make use of the maximum-likelihood estimation. Given that our continuous-time process estimation is relied on discretely sampled data and the fact that for some processes we use the density function is not known, we employ the likelihood expansion method of Ait-Sahalia (2002), who treats effectively the above problems. Alternative methods to the maximum-likelihood estimation for approximating parameters are solving numerically either the corresponding Fokker–Planck–Kolmogorov partial differential equation [e.g., see Lo (1988)] or simulation methods for large sample paths as in Pedeersen (1995). The method of Ait-Sahalia not only provides a closed form solution (so everything is computed analytically) but it has also been shown in Jensen and Poulsen (2002) to outperform such methods. [1]

---

[1] Walter Leal Filho • Vlasios Voudouris: Global Energy

In terms of a global economy, it is crystal clear that such a path is unsustainable. In other words, the current high consumption of natural resources will at some point in time reach the natural physical limits. Before this point, resources will become progressively scarcer and this will have several consequences, among which price increases are to be expected. However, the real world is more complicated than this and the market prices of minerals, and especially of fossil fuels, do not reflect their scarcity, and nor do they include external effects such as GHG emissions. Not surprisingly, they have fluctuated instead of steadily increasing with depletion and emissions and are now decreasing. Of course, technical progress has counteracted the scarcity effect on prices by making the extraction of more resources, in deeper layers or of less quality, possible. In a sense, the depletion effect has been totally or partially offset by the learning effect. This may appear a positive result for society, but the appearance is deceptive because emissions are not included in the prices. [1]

Within this line of thought—i.e. prices reflect scarcity of supply—the peak oil argument

---

Policy and Security. Springer-Verlag London 2013. P 156: 159

[1] Rossella Bardazzi • Maria Grazia Pazienza Alberto Tonini: European Energy and Climate Security. Springer International Publishing Switzerland 2016. P 164: 165

is one of the most popular. There is a vast literature on peak oil and different estimates are produced in terms of 'when' it will happen, but 2030 generally seems to be the year on which there is the most agreement. Thus, every time the oil price goes up there are people claiming that it is because the peak has been reached. In my view, peak oil is not that important because if we continue to burn it and we do not really adopt a plan to reduce its use and at some point, stop burning oil, the climate will be out of control. However, the attitude of "leave peak oil do" is not at all reassuring because it is another argument in favor of leaving the choice of energy sources to the market. It will stop using fossil fuels when their scarcity makes them non-economically viable, with no consideration whatsoever of the consequences for climate warming of reaching such a point. As Gerlagh has clearly pointed out, the problem is "too much oil" and not too little: some of it has to be left un-extracted if we really do care about climate change and therefore about the cumulative GHG emitted. Van der Ploeg has gone further and has estimated that "one trillion tons of carbon must be either left unused or be sequestrated".

To aggravate things further, the unconventional oil reserves recently discovered are as large as the conventional ones and this means that either substituting the un-conventional for conventional oil (as is the case with the US reduction in oil imports following the expansion of shale gas) or adding to the conventional oil will greatly aggravate climate warming, since unconventional oils are uncontroversially known to be more polluting than the conventional ones. Once again, we cannot adopt a policy of wait-and-see and react to market signals (prices), because they are flawed. We have already seen that they do not capture future scarcity and do not include external costs; otherwise, they would show an upward trend (in monetary and/or real terms) while they are now decreasing. [1]

The energy policy of the South Korean government aims at securing energy supply at low cost. The price of electricity, gas, and fuel are highly regulated by the government. Hence, the variable of price may fail to act as an applicable indicator for both demand and supply side of consumers and producers' responses to price changes. The energy demand will be determined by supply constraint not by the ordinary low of supply and demand. Countries such as South Korea that heavily rely on import for their energy use are mostly incorporating non-market-based mechanisms, rather than energy price to stabilize their local energy market. [2]

---

[1] Rossella Bardazzi • Maria Grazia Pazienza Alberto Tonini: European Energy and Climate Security. Springer International Publishing Switzerland 2016. P 165
[2] Nabaz T. Khayyat: Energy Demand in Industry. Springer

Energy prices and environmental problems are the major constraints on the development in different industries. Maximizing energy efficiency should be consistent with the public industrial development strategies. However, it is always not clear which choice will be made between pursuing greater intensive developments or less intensive strategies. This study will help to shed lights on how differently a certain policy affects each industry. [1]

Two key features drive markets' effectiveness. First, prices are an incredibly economical way to provide actors with information about the difficulty of delivering goods and services and about how much the goods or services are desired by others. If a firm wants to assess the difficulty of producing flour, it need look no further than the market price for flour.

If a firm wishes to gauge the willingness of consumers to acquire pencils, the market price of pencils is a supremely efficient indicator. When market conditions change, prices also change seamlessly, ensuring that market actors are continuously up-to-date about the market's fundamentals.

Science+Business Media Dordrecht 2015. P 8: 9
[1] Nabaz T. Khayyat: Energy Demand in Industry. Springer Science+Business Media Dordrecht 2015. P 193: 194

Without the price system, the firm wanting to assess the difficulty of producing flour must either conduct its own internal production experiments or issue surveys to flour producers. Both of these options are prohibitively time-consuming and/or expensive. The effectiveness of prices as a signal of the cost and value of products is most easily seen by considering the alternative: centralized planning. A central planner tasked with maximizing society's welfare is faced with the impossible task of gathering information from all individuals about their abilities and desires, and, after processing it, issuing instructions to each individual on what they need to do. This task is rendered doubly impossible by the fact that when fundamentals change, such as when a new technology is discovered, the central planner must reinitiate the information gathering process. The dramatic collapse of the former Soviet Union provides particularly stark evidence on the futility of such an endeavor.

The second key feature of markets is competition, which provides the incentives that ensure that prices reflect the underlying costs and values of goods, as well as motivating existing actors and entrants to develop new and superior products. A producer that understates its production cost will go bankrupt due to negative cash flow; a producer that overstates its production cost will go bankrupt due to lost market share. [1]

Despite their widespread success, markets are not universally effective. One of the biggest impediments to the correct functioning of a market is asymmetric information, whereby one party withholds non-price information that is relevant to the other party. For example, when seeking a loan from a bank, a prospective borrower can conceal information about what she plans to do with the money or about her fundamental entrepreneurial abilities. Unremedied, asymmetric information can lead to market unravelling, meaning a breakdown of trade.

Asymmetric information problems are not necessarily terminal for markets. Markets allow traders to build up reputations and the price system also incentivizes the appearance of intermediaries that can act as information brokers, such as the US company Consumer Reports. Such developments can lead to the rehabilitation of a market's effectiveness. However, the market does not always offer organic solutions to its problems, necessitating alternatives to the price system in some cases. 80

Oil prices have collapsed by more than half since July 2014. This drop-in energy prices came as a surprise to many observers. In the past, social and political insecurity, such as that experienced recurrently in the Middle East,

([1])Leo Lester: Energy Relations and Policy Making in Asia. 2016. P 79: 80

resulted in higher oil prices. But this time, despite instability in Libya, Iraq, and the Red Sea region, oil producers' revenues have plummeted.

Moreover, fallout from the Ukrainian crisis and the European Union and US implementation of sanctions against Russia have been further sources of geopolitical risk. Iran's potential return as an energy exporter will be progressive at best because of paramount technological limitations, and the country is unlikely to significantly contribute to supply in the short term. Despite these geopolitical trends, the decline in oil prices has continued unabated because of slower global economic growth and the resulting impact on energy demand, as well as a desire by Saudi Arabia in particular to maintain market share. Overall, such forces, when coupled with the heightened production stemming from US shale, have resulted in a supply glut. [1]

The new era of shale gas and tight oil and ongoing high Saudi Arabian oil production are the main reasons for the recent oil price collapse. The high oil prices experienced before the plunge made development of unconventional and untapped oil reserves, such as tar sands and shale oil in North America, commercially viable. But today, an oil price of $50–60 per barrel

---

[1] Leo Lester: Energy Relations and Policy Making in Asia. 2016. P 166

discourages private entrepreneurs from challenging the GCC's quasi-hegemony in energy production. The USA has now the potential to become energy self-sufficient and potentially also an energy exporter. Projections from BP indicate that the USA will need to import only 10 percent of its oil needs by 2035, and it is also emerging as a net natural gas exporter.

Similarly, in Canada, high oil prices have made it competitive to stop energy imports and instead exploit its large tar sands reserves. Even in a context of lower prices, large investments have been engaged and domestic production will likely continue. North America could become a competitive supplier that does not have to abide by artificial price mechanisms, such as OPEC production quotas. In terms of natural gas, the market effects of further LNG exports from Africa, the Levant, Russia, North America, and especially Australia, which is expected to emerge as the world's largest LNG exporter after 2020, could eventually produce a gas glut that mirrors the trend in the oil market. [1]

The sharp decline in oil prices also had an impact on the natural gas market, as natural gas prices on global markets are to some extent indexed to oil prices. However, the volatility of

---

[1] Leo Lester: Energy Relations and Policy Making in Asia. 2016. P 166: 167

natural gas prices is limited by the fact that major supply contracts are negotiated over long-term periods, while oil is largely sold on spot markets, which are much more vulnerable to speculative behaviors. The rapid oil price decline is therefore a major concern for all GCC countries, whether they produce mostly oil or gas, as their economies depend on energy revenue. One could even argue that North American unconventional production would have had a greater impact on prices without the sudden spike in gas demand triggered by the 2011 Fukushima disaster. As a result, Japan provided a substitute destination for displaced cargoes of LNG. Further ahead, increasing gas demand in China and India is expected to provide sizeable future contracts for Qatari LNG. Continued increases in US gas production could accentuate the interdependence between Asia and Qatar and encourage Qatar to further emphasize its economic linkages with the East. These market trends thus highlight Qatar's focus on prioritizing the Asian gas market ahead of its neighbors' needs. [1]

Due to the different types of energy used in the residential sector, mutual substitution is common. Therefore, what the people choose in terms of the type of energy is often the most cost-effective; namely, they compare the cost of

---

[1] Leo Lester: Energy Relations and Policy Making in Asia. 2016. P 167: 168

using different types of energy to produce the same result. When consuming energy, people always consider the cost-effective price of energy rather than its price per se. For example, when choosing between electricity and natural gas to heat water, they will consider the relative cost to boil the water. Hence, in the residential sector, the highest cost-effective price of the energy source has the greatest impact on total energy consumption.

Because the government has recently given financial subsidies on electricity, the prices of oil and gas are always relatively high (natural gas is not common). In the current stage, electricity has the highest cost performance. By using the Wind database, we can get the 2007 electricity prices in the different provinces. Then, according to the fuel price index from the "China Statistical Yearbook" and using the Brandt and Holz (2006) calculations in terms of PPP, we can calculate the provincial energy prices for the remaining years. [1]

In the US, the oil-gas industry is entirely private and cartels are illegal. Since the demise of the Texas Railroad Commission, there is no longer any government agency with the power to restrict output. Moreover, the US is still a net importer of oil, so low prices are

---

[1] Yi-Ming Wei • Hua Liao: Energy Economics: Energy Efficiency in China. Springer International Publishing Switzerland 2016. P 158

beneficial (on balance) to the rest of the economy. In the Russian economy, by comparison, exports of oil and gas are its life-blood. The low ruble means that imports are suddenly much more expensive, driving inflation. But there is an obvious way for Russia to escape from this bind, at least in the medium term: to increase sales to neighboring China. This requires a pipeline. The first steps toward a major bargain along these lines may have been taken in the last months.

Low prices will cut the hard currency income of both ISIS and Russia, as well as providing relief for European, South Asian, Japanese and Chinese consumers.

China and India are the major beneficiaries. Russia has been hurt the most. The Russian ruble has depreciated by more than 50% against the dollar, and inflation in Russia is now approaching 12% p.a.

The low prices will cut the profits of the big oil companies, but none will suffer greatly. It will also hurt some of the smaller energy companies, such as shale "frackers", especially those with heavy debt loads at high interest rates. The OPEC countries themselves will lose a lot of money but, except for Nigeria and Venezuela they can afford it. But, some analysts expect oil prices to be back over $80/bbl by next fall (2016), simply because the major OPEC exporters need the high prices to balance their budgets—and because the costs of drilling and fracking are very high and rising all the time. If OPEC cuts output to raise prices, as many hope, but few expect, the "plot" (if it is one) will probably have failed. [1]

The effects of changes in oil prices on economic activity receive a considerable amount of attention by economists and policymakers. Most of the studies assume that the relationship between oil prices and macroeconomic aggregates is linear and therefore, estimate it by using standard linear Vector Autoregressive (VAR) model and cointegration framework. However, it has been found that the decreases in the oil prices that take place after the second half of 1980s have smaller positive effects on economic activity than predicted by usual linear models.

Mork (1989) is the first study to provide the empirical evidence on asymmetric effects1 of oil price shocks on output. After this influential work, the asymmetric relationship between oil prices and economic aggregates has begun to gain importance. [2]

---

[1] Robert Ayres: ENERGY, COMPLEXITY AND WEALTH MAXIMIZATION. Springer International Publishing Switzerland 2016. P 318

[2] Yeliz Yalcin • Cengiz Arikan • Furkan Emirmahmutoglu: Determining the asymmetric effects of oil price changes on macroeconomic variables: a case study of Turkey. Springer

although the changes in oil prices increase the GDP growth, the cumulative effects of GDP decrease with the total effect of -0.3419 for 12 periods. This result is similar to the findings of Jones et al. (2004) and Lardic and Mignon (2008). The impacts of oil price shock on CPI and RER are positive, which is parallel to the literature. the oil price increases have larger impact on both GDP growth and inflation than the oil price declines. However, the negative oil price shocks have larger effect on RER than the positive oil price shocks. There are many reasons supporting these results for Turkey as an oil importer country. Since oil is a necessary good for Turkey and the share of oil in the budget is large, the negative oil price shocks have bigger impact on the exchange rate. Also, the taxes imposed by the government on oil prices increased the pump prices. This increase has further increased the exchange rate. [1]

Energy prices are one of the best tools for energy demand management. The objectives to be achieved by the governments in energy policies are mainly:

☐ Economically efficient pricing which promotes economic growth through efficient allocation of resources within the energy sector

Science+Business Media New York 2014. P 738
[1] Yeliz Yalcin • Cengiz Arikan • Furkan Emirmahmutoglu: Determining the asymmetric effects of oil price changes on macroeconomic variables: a case study of Turkey. Springer Science+Business Media New York 2014. P 744

and between the energy sectors the real economic costs of supplying energy.

☐ Promotion of social equity where governments often try to improve the situation of the poor price discrimination for demand categories will be faced.

☐ Resource mobilization both financially and fiscally government will maximize foreign exchange earnings through export or import substitution of energy sources (oil, coal and natural gas and in transformed form (fertilizers, methanol, fiscal resource mobilization is achieved by allowing producers and distributors of energy to recover their costs and to earn enough to finance their growth and development.

☐ Usage of energy resources for environment protection, i.e. repayment of oil products by natural gas will mitigate pollution Some of these objectives may conflict, e.g. social equity through subsidized prices may conflict with resource mobilization, so energy policy has to permit trade-off between different goals. It is more as art than the application of economic theory.

Short run marginal cost (SRMC) plus scarcity is hardly is hardly applied to less developing countries (LDC's) as a basin for energy pricing as it does not take into consideration long term needs of a growing economy.

Long term marginal cost (LRMC) is viewed as the best approximation for energy pricing. This is because also many investment projects in the oil and gas field are based on long term contracts which implies that the transmission capacity has already been sold before it is installed. LRMC pricing also fulfills the objective of resource mobilization in the sense that no subsidies are required. Other objectives such as life line rates for the poor and environment protection can lead to changes of the LRMC. But LRMC is difficult to implement because the determination of the correct LRMC for different types of consumers is often not possible. The average incremental cost (AIC) can be used to estimate the LRMC. Fully distributed cost (FDC) pricing needs more information.

Since natural gas is a depletable resource, depletion allowance (DA) has to be included in the economic cost of natural gas to adjust for the consumption foregone. It depends on price of replacement fuel for the gas used, whose value depends on LNG price. Offshore and onshore purchase gas prices have to be considered. [1]

---

[1] PROF. DR. ENG H. FARAG/ ENG. A, ELMISSIRIEGUIDELINES FOR EVALUATION OF NATURAL GAS PROJECTS. P 4: 6

The great uncertainty in all issues of forecasting and the creation of scenarios can be nicely seen in retrospect in the work of GWS (2003) and Distelkamp et al. (2003).

The economic model, PANTA RHEI, had to be fed with oil price assumptions for scenarios up until 2020. The assumption made in 2003 was that the oil price would remain between $22–28 per barrel. This was essentially a no-change forecast. Now, some 10 years later, it is (too) easy to see with the help of hindsight that there three "mistakes" were made: (1) the level is much higher in 2012—about $100— instead of $25; (2) the higher level has been achieved through a (temporary) positive growth rate rather than a jump of prices; (3) fluctuations and their potential increase seem not to have been taken into account. In short, the no-change forecast was wrong and scenarios of increasing oil prices were not simulated. Later studies, listed in Table 5.2, adjusted their forecast to contain the recently observed growth rates, which began increasing after 1999. What should be emphasised here is the great uncertainty inherent to such forecasts. The underlying problem can be understood through efforts to find trends of oil prices denoted as P in the following. Bernard et al. (2012) estimated several variants of Pindyck's (1999) autoregressive model:

$$\ln P = a + bt + c \ln P(-1) + u(t)$$

Here a, b, and c are coefficients to be estimated, t is a time trend and u is an error term, which is the vertical distance of the observations from the regression line.

Using this model and its time-varying coefficients, the authors found growth rates for gas prices of about 4–6 % and for oil prices of about 9–10 % for data until 1996.

When using forecasting criteria for 1976–2006, these results and methods are roughly confirmed with the exception of the real-time price of oil. For the real-time oil price forecast, though, the specification of a random walk without drift, obtained by setting a = b = 0, c = 1 and getting $\ln P = \ln P(-1) + u(t)$, works best, implying an expected value of a no-change forecast as in GWS (2003), which could justify to some extent the assumption made there. For the long run of 30 years, however, the other models that perform best in the estimates are confirmed. By combining these results, and having referred to Pindyck's (1999) paper, one could have come to

Table 5.2 Assumptions of oil price increases in energy models

Study	Period	Real oil price percentage growth rate
GWS (2003)	2003–2010	0
Schlesinger et al. (2010)	2008–2050	0.8 %
Nitsch et al. (2010)	2010–2050	0.56–1.47 % (crude); 0.8–2.3 % (mineral)
Schlesinger et al. (2011)	2008–2030	0.7–2.9 %
Lehr et al. (2011)	2009–2030	0.1–6 %
Nitsch et al. (2012)	2010–2050	1.2–1.9 %

expect, around the year 2000, that in the long run, there would be a positive growth in oil prices. Making several scenarios rather than relying on stationarity would have been adequate.

The general impression of increasing oil prices is therefore not necessarily true. This can be seen from a mere look at the data for real and nominal oil prices in Figs. fits the general impression of increasing oil prices since the first oil crisis in 1973. But the increase in real prices in the Figure is very different. In 1999, the oil price was back to its 1949 level. Indeed, Pindyck's (1999) estimates did not give much reason to expect increasing real oil prices. It was only after 1999 that real oil prices increased. But this was not known in 1999, and today it is not known whether these prices will continue to rise or whether they will fall again, as after 1983. The expectation of increasing oil prices is also based on the idea of limited resources, such as the peak-oil idea. But this idea does not tell us when oil prices will increase and by how much, which is essential information for planning investments. Moreover, technical change in the finding, exploiting, and use of oil may happen faster than the growth of other components of demand for oil. In this theoretical case, a growth in oil prices may not occur. Theory alone cannot clarify this, as it is an empirical issue. The question that has lingered since

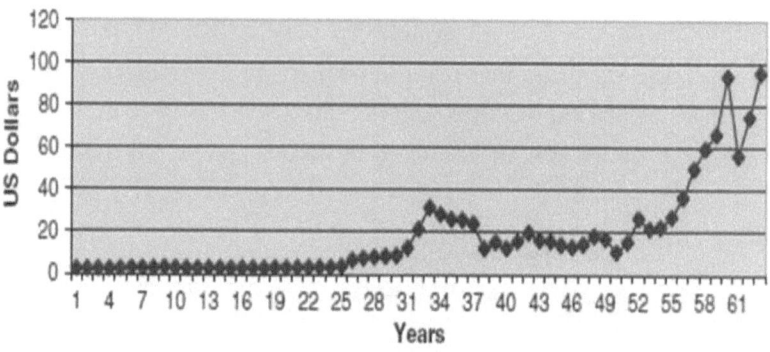

Fig. 5.1 Nominal oil prices 1949–2011

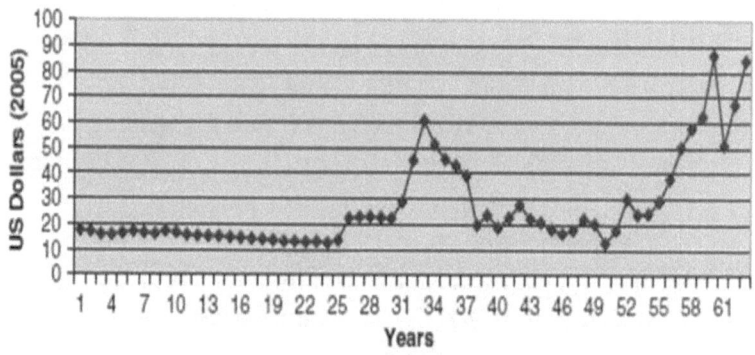

Fig. 5.2 Real oil prices 1949–2011

Pindyck's (1999) paper therefore is whether or not it is a random walk. This question is now considered from the perspective of the GARCH and VECM models. We prefer to use our own estimates rather than drawing on the literature alone. This is because less recent papers have a much shorter sub-period of data availability for the rise of oil prices after 1999 and do not provide long-term forecasts; instead, they mainly discuss the methods, with exceptions among those discussed above and listed in the first table of this section.

The necessary theoretical background for both of these is the standard supply demand model. The relation of the model to oil prices is that observed oil prices, as they appear in our data, are the result of the equilibrium of supply and demand.

Supply and demand both depend on the price of oil. When prices are higher, firms incur higher costs and supply larger quantities, but consumers and firms buy less.

An additional argument driving demand for oil is household income and production of firms. If consumers have a higher income, they demand more heating oil and gasoline for their vehicles, both of which are based on oil. As consumers' demand for other goods also increases, firms produce more and demand a greater oil input. If consumers in foreign countries have a higher income, they also demand more oil.

International competition for oil drives up the price. The large users of oil are the rich countries, but poorer countries also demand more oil if their income is higher over the business cycle, or if it grows over time. Moreover, supply functions are closely related to cost function. Cost functions increase through growing prices of factors such as wages, but they decrease through technical change in the finding and exploiting of resources. While at the macro level these two effects roughly balance each other out, this does not need to be the case at the sector level. Similarly, on the demand side, the prices of substitutes for, and complements of, oil may increase or decrease relative to the price of oil, thereby shifting the demand function. Expected future prices may come into play on the supply and the demand side. Investment, allowing optimal inventory, shifts the demand function higher while technical change in using oil shifts the demand to lower quantities. We have captured all of these trends over the past decades by using a time trend variable, which also captures the trend part of the income terms. In addition, unexpected effects enter as a stochastic term on the supply and the demand side to the extent that they are not dampened by inventory policies.

Equating supply to demand eliminates the quantities and results in prices as a function of the income terms. He et al. (2010) has provided a simple formal elaboration of the model without the time trend variable and using Kilian's (2009) economic activity index instead of income variables. [1]

1.1. WORLD ENERGY POLICY

It is important to clarify from the beginning that a short cut is not being sought by using a simplistic model where the financial speculation is soley responsible for all the chaos in the oil market. The financial investments are likely just taking advantage of the existing paradoxes and bottlenecks in the oil industry and in the energy policy worldwide.

The stability will eventually come only when and if these structural problems are solved.

For the time being we are just observing further additional elements of crisis arriving and making the scenario even worse. The North Africa crisis (Libya in particular) and the Fukushima nuclear accident are referred to.

These two events will amplify the structural crisis of the oil market, accelerating all

---

[1] Bert Droste-Franke • Martin Carrier Matthias Kaiser • Miranda Schreurs Christoph Weber • Thomas Ziesemer: Improving Energy Decisions. Springer International Publishing Switzerland 2015. P 158: 160

the processes already in progress since the Chernobyl accident.

We have already experienced in all the industrialized countries the lack of an energy policy that is capable of harmonizing the growing energy demand with the new respect for the environment. The development of environmental regulations in the last two decades has created burdensome (but unchallengeable) limits for the energy and oil companies in particular but has not driven the bodies concerned to make the investments necessary to create 'compliant' energy and products.

The result of these divergent processes has been the net reduction of availability of finished products marketable in the western industrialized countries. There is now a shortage of clean gasoline and gasoil.

In total the shortfall in the USA amounts to about 50 million tons per year of gasoline, and about 40 million tons per year of gasoil in Europe. To bridge these gaps, it is necessary to import from other geographical areas, which obviously deprives local consumers of these products or forces them to pay the higher prices that consumers in the strong countries can pay to get their hands on the missing products. It is a real competition where the winners are always the ones who can pay more.

A glance at the newspapers is enough to discover the limitations imposed on motorists in Middle Eastern countries (Iran, Egypt etc.) or all of West Africa.

The deficit of these high-quality finished products has bolstered the rise in crude oil prices, particularly the light varieties such as those from the North Sea or North Africa. Somewhat similar to what would happen if, for some strange reason, a rule was introduced to allow the sale of only choice cuts of meat (fillet steak, entrec^ote, silverside): the price of these would rise but so would the price of the cow.

This potential shortage of finished products has spread the feeling in the trading market that something is at risk and, on a daily basis, somebody may not be able to get the product he or she is looking for.

The oil market has become nervous and very transient, with the same level of volatility experienced during the Gulf wars (when the risk of a shortage of supply was evident).

The recent dramatic events (Fukushima and Libya) will definitely amplify the already existing concerns and tensions and will spread the sensitivity about the environmental issues worldwide and accelerate the increase of the demand for clean products.

We cannot forget that the only decision taken at the global political level in one of the G20 meetings, to reduce the impact on the economy of the increasing price of oil, was to encourage the construction of new nuclear plants for producing electricity. This decision was inadequate already when it was taken (less than 10% of the oil is used to produce electricity) but today, after Fukushima, it appears to be almost obsolete.

We can say without any doubt that there is a lack of energy policy worldwide, but especially in the industrialized countries; only China and India are building what they need, despite the apparent general market indication.

The world oil market is already in the middle of these tensions, but we have not yet seen the worst. The forthcoming summers will offer some anticipation of the future developments we can expect in the near future, with a shortage of supply of high-quality gasoline and clean gasoil and a significant increase of the price differential between light and heavy crude oils.

Later the combined impact of the reduction of the sweet light crude oils (like the ones produced by Libya) and the shortage of clean products will be examined with more technical detail and analysis. An understanding will be gained as to why Saudi Arabia was ready to increase the production to compensate the reduction of supply from Libya, but, after a couple of weeks had to stop producing additional barrels of oil.

The quality (more than the quantity) of the crude oils offered to the market is today a crucial factor for meeting the demand of products worldwide. With the existing quality of the raw materials, it takes new technologies and massive investments in the refinery industry. We are far away from implementing such solutions worldwide.

It is evident that the structural problems for the oil industry will remain as they are in the next decade and they will keep providing grounds for financial speculation and therefore for the increase of prices, as has happened in the last ten years. [1]

1.2. Energy Demand

The demand for energy is defined as: a derived demand that arises for satisfying some needs which are met through use of appliances.

According to this definition, the energy demand depends on the type of energy chosen to be used in a device for a process or activity, in

---

[1] Salvatore Carollo: Understanding Oil Prices A John Wiley & Sons, Ltd., Publication. 2012. P 8:10

which it will be influenced by the price of the chosen energy type, the price of the device used by the energy type, the availability of the devise used, and other factors such as environmental conditions, decision maker's preferences, income, demand for energy substitutes, etc. Accordingly, changes in the demand for energy depend mainly on the supply of the device used. Thus, response to the change will lead to inflexible results, as changes in response to the changes in supply of the device might be influenced by factors other than energy demand. The supply of the device used depends mainly on a set of characteristics such as device cost, availability, and efficiency. [1]

The response to change in the energy demand is partially characterized and explained by changes in the behavior of the decision maker. Thus, the elasticity of energy that respond to changes in the short run is incomplete, while in the long run will be accumulated over time and fully captured. The short run elasticity will depend on the output level, while in the long run other factors in addition to the level of output will determine the size of the elasticity such as taxes, prices, technical progress, changes in the industry structure, and policies toward more efficient use of energy.

---

[1] Nabaz T. Khayyat: Energy Demand in Industry. Springer Science+Business Media Dordrecht 2015. P 39

Factors that derive the demand for energy by industries are determined based on the production theory with a priori expected outcome. These factors are different by industries as well as over time. Energy is considered as an input in the production, and hence, the cost minimization approach is applied when the firm is maximizing the profit.

The cost minimization and profit maximization goals of the producer in the industrial sector are subjected to a number of restrictions such as the production process and its capacity in producing maximum quantity of output given the level of inputs available and used, the fixed capacity of the firm during a certain time period, price and availability of different inputs used in the production process, and the price of their substitutes. The factor demand functions can be derived from the cost minimization approach, which aims at producing units of outputs up to the level that the rate of technical substitution will be equal to the price of the inputs used.

1.3. The Elasticity of Demand

The elasticity can be defined as responsiveness of the dependent variable to changes in the explanatory variables. It is a measure of changes in explanatory variables that affect the dependent variable. If the left and right-hand side variables are expressed in logarithmic form, all the variables then can be in different units of measurement, and yet the changes will express percentage changes, or elasticities. The elasticity is defined as if an explanatory variable such as materials use increases with one percent, how many percent the demand for energy will be changed, ceteris paribus (meaning everything else unchanged). [1]

1.4. Energy Efficiency

Improving the energy efficiency is one of the most important objectives of energy policy and strategy in all countries. Coping with United Nations Framework Convention on Climate Change (UNFCCC) is a big challenge for many countries and their industries. Given the nature of various production processes and technologies used, some industries use more energy than others. South Korea has a high level of dependency on imported energy. The share of imported primary energy in the overall energy supply is high so that improvement in energy use efficiency is the most powerful and cost-effective way of meeting the objectives of environmentally sustainable development strategy. Furthermore, it can reduce the high fossil fuels dependency by achieving a higher energy efficiency level. [2]

---

[1] Nabaz T. Khayyat: Energy Demand in Industry. Springer Science+Business Media Dordrecht 2015. P 39: 41
[2] Nabaz T. Khayyat: Energy Demand in Industry. Springer Science+Business Media Dordrecht 2015. P 27

Energy use efficiency is an important issue due to limit in replacing the energy factor with other substitutable factors. South Korean's dependence on energy sources from overseas is maintained at about 97 % since 2000. Energy efficiency is weighty part regarding policy formulation and evaluation, as it is evidenced and convincing that improving energy efficiency is the best way to achieve energy security and to reduce greenhouse gas emission.

The main objectives of the South Korean energy policy are sustainability, high security, and competitiveness of the energy supply. Efficient use of energy can be a solution to cope with the desired reductions in emission of greenhouse gases (GHG) and effects on climate change. In order to design effective energy policies, it is necessary to have information on energy demand, its price, and consumer responses in forms of various elasticities. These can be used to monitor the progress in the energy use. A typical indicator is energy intensity to set up energy policy. This is emphasized by a report from the International Energy Agency on the Energy Efficiency Policies in the G8 (extended recently to G20). According to the report many countries have shown improved energy efficiency which is explained by the decrease in energy intensity since the 1970s. The recent civil unrest in the Middle East and subsequent increase in the oil price are two other reminders of the importance of energy security for a highly energy dependent industrialized country such as South Korea. [1]

Energy efficiency is relevant to energy exporters as well. Energy producing countries are concerned about maintaining or increasing production levels to meet the growing domestic demand brought about by a rapidly increasing population and a growing economy. Thus, many governments in energy-producing countries are introducing energy efficiency initiatives and programs. [2]

The combination of all these factors makes energy efficiency relevant to the world. The International Energy Agency (IEA) declared in its World Energy Outlook 2012 that energy efficiency should be considered as the 'other' source of energy; energy efficiency improvements allow the meeting of end-use demand with less energy supply. IEA predicts that energy efficiency measures will drive a reduction in CO_2 emissions, accounting for more than two-thirds of the cumulative global reduction in energy-related CO_2 emissions by 2035. Energy efficiency simply makes sense for every country. [3]

---

[1] Nabaz T. Khayyat: Energy Demand in Industry. Springer Science+Business Media Dordrecht 2015. P 27
[2] Leo Lester: Energy Relations and Policy Making in Asia. 2016. P 289: 290
[3] Leo Lester: Energy Relations and Policy Making in Asia. 2016. P 290: 291

Improvements in energy efficiency have long been recognized as a key element of policies focused on reducing emissions. Therefore, an alternative sensitivity – Accelerated Efficiency (AE) case – was developed assuming somewhat more aggressive efficiency improvements than those incorporated in the Reference Case. It is important to note, however, that the rates of efficiency improvements assumed in the AE case do not fully explore the potential for improvement that exists in the oil sector. On the contrary, they in fact represent the moderate levels that are plausibly achievable if policymakers and technology work together in an orchestrated way in the decades to come.

Compared to the Reference Case, the overall demand reduction in the AE case is 3.2 mb/d by 2040. The larger part of this reduction, around two thirds, is assumed to take place in Developing countries where a higher potential for efficiency improvements exists. Assumed efficiency improvements in China would translate into some 0.6 mb/d lower oil demand than in the Reference Case while India contributes another 0.3 mb/d. Because of the high overall level of oil demand in the group of Other DCs, the potential demand reduction in this region is more than 1 mb/d. The corresponding demand decline in Eurasia and OECD is 0.2 mb/d and 0.9 mb/d, respectively.

These estimates clearly show that the net effect of an orchestrated push for even moderate improved efficiencies across all sectors of oil demand is comparable to the impact of alternative economic developments, as well as to the much-discussed impact of a potential faster penetration of electric vehicles. [1]

Historically, energy policy decision making in market economies has often been based on mainstream economic theory, which in turn relies on fundamental assumptions such as the availability of perfect information to both buyers and sellers, zero transaction costs, and complete rationality on the part of market participants. Mainstream economic theory distinguishes among market failures/imperfection, and market barriers. The existence of market failures/imperfections may justify public policy intervention if the intervention passes a cost–benefit analysis. Brown (2001) writes: "the existence of market failures and barriers that inhibit socially optimal levels of investment in energy efficiency is the primary reason for considering public policy interventions. In many instances, feasible low-cost policies can be implemented that either eliminate or compensate for market imperfections and barriers, enabling markets to operate more efficiently to the benefit of society. In other instances, policies may not be feasible;

---

[1] http://www.opec.org/opec_web/en/index.htm

they may not fully eliminate the targeted barrier or imperfection; or they may do so at costs that exceeds the benefits.

In other words, barriers to energy efficiency that can be classified as market failures/imperfections may lead to policy adoption, while so-called market barriers—which include any barrier accounting for the energy efficiency gap—cannot justify policy adoption. The classification of barriers clearly has great implications for whether, how, and when a policy should be adopted. [1]

For enhanced energy efficiency potential to be realized, policy makers must include energy management in policies. Can policy options help improve energy management practices and promote the adoption of energy efficiency measures, boosting energy efficiency and taking us toward improved sustainability? Insights from the book regarding the efficacy of policy instruments are discussed in the next section referring to the energy policy gap. [2]

---

[1] Patrik Thollander • Jenny Palm: Improving Energy Efficiency in Industrial Energy Systems. Springer-Verlag London 2013. P 36

[2] Patrik Thollander • Jenny Palm: Improving Energy Efficiency in Industrial Energy Systems. Springer-Verlag London 2013. P 143

1.5. World Economy and Energy Consumption Are Significantly Correlated

In the late 20th century, the aggregate economic elasticity of demand for energy showed a decreasing trend. The major reason was that the economic growth rate in the developing countries was only slightly higher (1–2 %) than that in the developed countries in the last 50 years of the century. From the composition of world energy demand, we can see that the low growth rate in the developed countries somewhat softened the high growth rate in the developing countries, lowering the growth rate of world energy demand and reducing the energy elasticity. Since 2001, the sharp economic growth in the developing countries (almost 4 % higher than that in the developed countries) has driven the rapid increase in energy demand, which could not be completely offset by the lower growth rate of energy demand in the developed countries. Thus, the energy elasticity of demand showed an upward trend during this period. [1]

With economic restructuring and technological progress, most countries and regions in the world have shown a decreasing trend in energy consumption per unit of GDP

---

[1] Yi-Ming Wei • Hua Liao: Energy Economics: Energy Efficiency in China. Springer International Publishing Switzerland 2016. P 4

since 1980 while some other countries have shown an increasing trend periodically. From 1980 to 2008, energy consumption per unit of GDP in the United States decreased by 44 % and that in Japan decreased by 23 %. For the developing countries, India decreased by 19 % and China decreased by 66 %. The sharp decrease in China played a positive role in relieving global energy demand and greenhouse gas (GHG) emissions. The energy consumption per unit of GDP in South Africa and Brazil showed an increasing trend from 1980 to 2000 before slowing down after 2000. Some major developing countries have great potential in reducing their energy consumption, improving their technologies and shifting to less energy-intensive industries in the near future. To realize these objectives, more specific and enforceable strategic planning is needed. [1]

Triggered by the world economy recession, global energy demand slumped substantially in 2009. global energy demand decreased by 1.1 % in 2009. The IEA (2010b) showed that global oil demand was 84.94 million barrels per day (bbl/d) in 2009, a decrease of 1.5 % from the previous year. Oil demand in the OECD countries was 45.49 million bbl/d, a decrease of 4.4 %, while that in China was 7.89 million bbl/d, an increase of 7.7

---

[1] Yi-Ming Wei • Hua Liao: Energy Economics: Energy Efficiency in China. Springer International Publishing Switzerland 2016. P 4: 5

%, and that in other countries was 30.77 million bbl/d, an increase of 0.6 %. The second quarter of 2009 was the slowest period in recent years in terms of energy demand, with a daily demand of 84.1 million barrels. The expected global oil demand was 86.5 million bbl/d in 2010, with a growth rate of 1.8 % from the previous year. The global electricity consumption decreased by 1.6 % in 2009, the first negative growth rate since World War II. [1]

The historical background, resource endowment, economic strength, and stage of development of the different countries vary substantially. The US, UK, France, Japan, Germany, Italy, and Canada are the member states of the former "Group of Seven" (G7) and they are major industrialized countries. The G7 countries play a significant role in the global economic, political, and energy fields, with 53 % of the world's total GDP (2008, rate method) and 34 % of the world's total energy consumption (2007). The historical experiences and lessons learned from energy development in the G7 countries provide plenty of useful references for the developing countries. China, India, Brazil, and Russia (generally called the "BRICs") are the most important developing countries as well as emerging market countries. These four countries are experiencing rapid

---

[1] Yi-Ming Wei • Hua Liao: Energy Economics: Energy Efficiency in China. Springer International Publishing Switzerland 2016. P 14

growth and they not only have large economies, but they are also playing an increasingly important role in the international community. The combined GDP of these countries account for 14 % of the world's total (2008, rate method) and their energy consumption amounts to 29 % of the world's total (2007). In addition, their proportions of incremental economy and energy in the world's total incremental economy and energy are even higher. [1]

    Natural gas is priced and traded as a commodity at different locations throughout the country. These locations are known as market hubs that are normally located at the intersection of major pipeline systems. The biggest market hub is Henry Hub located in Louisiana, and the spot and future natural gas prices set at Henry Hub are generally considered as the primary price set for the North American natural gas market. Depending on the specific usage, the natural gas consumption can be classified into three major partitions, including lease and plant fuel, pipeline and distribution use, and volumes delivered to consumers. There are four types of end-customers, namely power plants, industrial customers, commercial customers, and residential customers. [2]

---

[1] Yi-Ming Wei • Hua Liao: Energy Economics: Energy Efficiency in China. Springer International Publishing Switzerland 2016. P 18
[2] Georgios M. Kopanos · Pei Liu Michael C. Georgiadis: Advances in Energy Systems Engineering. Springer

On 11 March 2011, a devastating earthquake caused a radiation leak at the Japanese nuclear plant Fukushima. In response to the nuclear reactor crisis in Japan, industrialized European nations immediately questioned the nuclear future of their economies. The German Chancellor Angela Merkel was the first political leader to commit to the suspension of multiple nuclear reactors in the country. Her announcement caused an instantaneous jump in carbon prices. Speculation over the increased demand for coal in the face of future reductions in nuclear energy output gave rise to a significant increase in the price of carbon allowances. Such evidence from the market seems to suggest that market participants are able to accurately price in new information. The aim of this study is to empirically investigate if, and to what extent, the carbon market is efficient. An event study methodology is employed to examine if new information reaching the market affects the expected price of carbon futures contracts, thereby causing abnormally positive or negative returns. [1]

International Publishing Switzerland 2017. P 26
[1] Yulia Veld-Merkoulova • Svetlana Viteva: Carbon Finance. Springer International Publishing Switzerland 2016. P 19: 20

1.6. The Economic Drivers of the Political Will for Social Responsibility in Energy Policy for Fossil Fuel Exporting Countries

Over the long-term the evidence shows that there are significant equilibrium relationships between political risk, domestic stock market prices, global benchmark stock market prices and global oil and gas prices, particularly in the period following the global financial crisis. When the full period is considered these relationships are strongest for Canada, Kuwait, the UAE, the UK and the US. It is clear that in the long-term and particularly after the onset of the GFC that domestic and global economic factors, as reflected in stock market prices and oil and gas prices, have much to do with levels of political risk and thus they have much to do with changes in the level of political will and areas that are affected by political will such as domestic and global perceptions of social responsibility. [1]

This is contrary to theory, where political risk ratings are related only to political factors as assessed subjectively by international political risk ratings experts. Generally speaking there is no strong relationship in the long-term (over the full period and in the period leading up

---

[1] Andre' Dorsman • O" zgєur Arslan-Ayaydin • Mehmet Baha Karan: Energy and Finance. Springer International Publishing Switzerland 2016. P 160

to the GFC) in Venezuela between risk ratings and economic data and it is therefore likely that political factors played an important part in ascribed risk ratings for that country (at levels that reflect higher political risk and lower levels of political will and social responsibility).

In the short-term Granger causality tests do not, in most cases, identify significant and specific exogenous variables, however, it may be assumed, in the cases where cointegration exists, that collectively there is a degree of either one way or dual Granger causality as the variables all interact in a single model and they together come to equilibrium at least once over the periods studied. [1]

It is clear from cointegration evidence, rather than evidence of exogeneity, that in most cases over the pre-and post-crisis period, domestic and international economic factors have a degree of influence on political risk. In developing countries generally, these economic factors influence higher levels of political risk and therefore lower levels of political will for socially responsible energy policies. In general, in developed countries these same factors influence lower levels of political risk and perhaps show greater political will to implement socially responsible energy policies.

---

[1] Andre´ Dorsman • O¨ zgєur Arslan-Ayaydin • Mehmet Baha Karan: Energy and Finance. Springer International Publishing Switzerland 2016. P 160

Over the long-term, in higher political risk countries, it is expected that there is a possibility that there is less political will to implement policies for social responsibility in fossil fuel exports and that economic factors are important purely as drivers of wealth in export and GDP growth. In developed countries there is less political risk and economic factors are expected to be important as drivers of wealth so that socially responsible policies (such as those relating to the use of renewable energy sources) can become affordable and can be placed on government policy agendas with some degree of certainty that they will be implemented in due course (for example, the joining of international agreements to reduce greenhouse gas emissions over a time span to a certain level). [1]

1.7. Crude Oil Pricing

Before World War II, the world oil market (mainly the United States, the world's largest producer, consumer, and a net exporter) was controlled by the major oil companies. Thus, the single basing-point price system was applied. Under this system the price is quoted only for the point of delivery. It equaled the f.o.b. price at the base, which was the U.S. coast of the Gulf of Mexico, plus transport and insurance costs to its destination. This system

---

[1] Andre´ Dorsman • O¨ zg€ur Arslan-Ayaydin • Mehmet Baha Karan: Energy and Finance. Springer International Publishing Switzerland 2016. P 161

tended to prevent competition and lower prices. After the war and the emergence of new suppliers from the Middle East, the price structure changed to a dual basing point system. The second basing point was the Arabian Gulf. By this system Middle Eastern oil was priced based on f.o.b. prices from the Arabian Gulf, which were agreed upon by the company and producing governments as equal to f.o.b. U.S. Gulf parity prices plus the transport cost from the Arabian Gulf to destination. This was about equivalent to the U.S. Gulf price plus the transport cost from some point near Malta in the Mediterranean. With the increase in demand for Middle Eastern crude oil, especially in Western Europe, oil companies moved the "parity point" westward to London, then to New York, in order to maintain low competitive prices among the various producer countries exporting to Europe.

In the 1950s, real oil prices tended to decline, except for the years 1956 to 1957 when the Suez Canal was closed. In this atmosphere of price volatility, OPEC was formed in 1960. The two-basing-point system was abandoned, at least for crude oil. Yet OPEC did not succeed in stabilizing oil prices and preventing them from falling. OPEC's first effective attempt to raise prices in line with demand growth and inflation took place in February 1971, when the Tehran agreement was signed. As a result of this agreement, the price of 40° API Arabian Gulf crude increased by 33 ¢/bbl plus 2 q/bbl in settlement of freight disparities.

Until that time, oil prices were posted by the major integrated oil companies. However, these were realized or market selling prices, which were determined by giving discounts of posted prices. The posted prices, however, served as a basis for oil-producing governments to calculate their royalty interests and income taxes from the oil companies operating in their countries. OPEC was able to seize the initiative, and official OPEC prices emerged.

After October 1973 (34° API)—as a marker crude—Saudi Arabia light became OPEC's official reference crude oil. OPEC set a price for Saudi Arabia light and let member governments set their own prices for the different crudes reflecting the different locational, physical, and chemical characteristics of each crude.

Supply disruption from the Arabian Gulf because of the Iran Revolution in 1979–1980 caused spot oil prices to jump to over $40/bbl and official prices of OPEC's crudes to rise accordingly. In the early 1980s, spot and future markets were widely used at the same time. In those conditions spot and official prices declined. This led OPEC members to follow market-based pricing systems. In February 1987, OPEC effectively terminated market-priced sales, and oil prices tended to stabilize around a target price of $18/bbl as OPEC's reference basket price or oil-pricing benchmark.

The current basket is composed of 12 crudes: Algerian Sahara blend, Angola's Girassol, Ecuador's Oriente, Iran's heavy, Iraq's Basra light, Kuwait's export, Libya's Essider, Nigeria's Bonny light, Qatar's Marine, Saudi Arabia's Arab light, United Arab Emirates' Murban, and Venezuela's Merey. Theoretically, this is a return to fixed price system. However, in March 2000, the reference basket price was set at a range of $22 to $28/bbl to reflect market forces. The market-based pricing system was enhanced by the development of derivative instruments such as forwards, futures options, and swaps. Trading oil became either through paper markets, where deals are futures and swaps, or physical oil trading through spot market and long-term contracts, where the price of a cargo in long-term contracts is linked to spot price. Such financial and electronic revolutions caused massive market speculation and more fluctuation in oil prices. The period from 1990 to 2010 witnessed a wide variation in the exchange value of the U.S. dollar, which increased the volatility of oil prices. Beyond oil supply and demand, the effect of the U.S. dollar as the oil pricing currency and the increased role of paper trading of oil have substantially changed the structure of the oil market. [1]

At this stage of the introduction to crude oil science and technology and in keeping with the historical aspects that have been discussed earlier, a word (or two) about crude oil pricing and the historical perspectives is warranted.

Currently, oil is the primary energy source in the world. For a century, the world has depended on low-cost oil to stimulate and maintain economic growth. However, sustaining the rate of economic growth is open to question because the volume of oil that can ultimately be recovered is subject to much speculation because of the uncertainties of reserve estimation and this, in turn, affects the price of oil.

At this stage, while dealing with petroleum reserves and resources, it is appropriate to deal with a related topic and that is crude oil prices. However, it is not the intent here to move into predictions of the future. There is nothing difficult about making predictions. But accurate predictions of future events are always difficult! It is difficult to be correct! Everyone can justify with amazingly accurate 20–20 hindsight why their predictions were incorrect. But they are never incorrect. These erstwhile mediums will use statistics to show that, after several rounds of mathematical

---

[1]Hussein K. Abdel-Aal, Mohammed A. Alsahlawi: Petroleum Economics and Engineering. Third Edition. Taylor & Francis Group, LLC. 2014. P 33:34

manipulation, their predictions were very close. Even though the outcome bears no relationship to what really happened. It is easy to make a statement that oil prices will continue to rise (after all, the pessimist is never disappointed), but the predictability lies in determining when and by how much. [1]

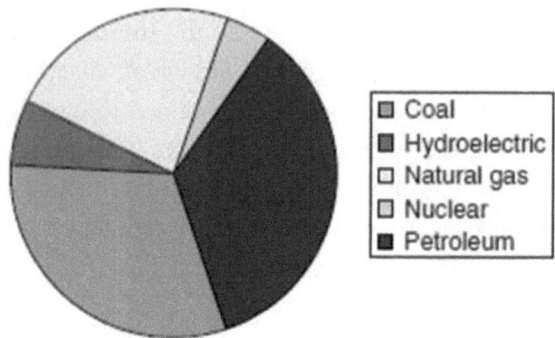

From 1949 until the end of 1970, Middle East crude oil prices had averaged about $1.90 per barrel. But on October 16th of that year, OPEC members meeting in Vienna suddenly decided to boost oil and gas prices by 70 percent, from $3.01 per barrel to $5.11. The following day, the Arab members—Saudi Arabia, Kuwait, Iraq, Libya, Abu Dhabi, Qatar, and Algeria—announced that they were going to cut their production below the September level by 5 percent for October and an additional 5

---

[1]James G. Speight: The Chemistry and Technology of Petroleum. FOURTH EDITION. Taylor & Francis Group, LLC. 2007. P 60

percent per month, "until Israeli withdrawal is completed from the whole Arab territories occupied in June 1967 and the legal rights of the Palestinian people are restored."

OPEC had the West over a barrel, and within a year, the majors had lost whatever control they had over pricing. Oil prices quadrupled, generating the world's first "oil shock," which rocked the global economy. The resulting energy crisis hit Europe and North America hard, with long lineups at filling stations and rapidly inflating prices.

The energy poker game that followed OPEC's announcement would change the world utterly and give fresh impetus to the development of the Sands. [1]

The survival of an enterprise or business is greatly dependent on its pricing policy, which also influences the balanced growth of both consumption and supply. The pricing decision is mostly the outcome of satisfying and balancing a number of issues including economic, business environment, business maturity and health, and other specificities. The price is a determinant of revenue, which a firm usually seeks to maximize. As mentioned earlier, price fixation is a delicate issue that is influenced by numerous

---

[1] Alastair Sweeny: Black Bonanza. John Wiley & Sons Canada, Ltd. 2010. P 108

internal and external factors. The internal factors are predominantly cost management policy including operational, commercial, and financial aspects. The cost is a major determinant factor and indicator of price—it specifies the boundary or resistance point to the lowering of price beyond which the product is not economical or business is not sustainable. The potential external factors are elasticity of supply and demand, competition, company goodwill, purchasing power of buyers, entry barrier, and government policy.

The factors influencing pricing of different commodities are generally not the same. Even the factors influencing pricing of the same commodity may vary from country to country or market to market. Pricing is not an exact science nor does it follow any particular economic model, even though it is influenced by the economic factors. Pricing is more of a judgment based on sound economic principles and reliable information. There is no infallible formula for determining the right price for a product. Every pricing situation is unique and should be explored based on its distinctiveness.

Pricing assumes significance, especially when a new product is launched or when a product enters a new market competing with an existing product. The factors that are generally considered for determining prices of commodities are maximization of profit, promotion of product, long-range welfare and policies, adoptability and flexibility to meet change, price sensitivity, conflicting interests of manufacturer and middlemen, active entry of nonbusiness groups, market penetration, market skimming, early cash recovery, and so on. Needless to say, there are multitudes of forces, causes, and factors that influence pricing of a product. Accordingly, pricing strategy is categorized as follow:

•• *Price elasticity of demand*: It is the ratio of percentage change in demand to percentage change in price. The degree of price elasticity impacts the level of sales and revenue. If the demand is inelastic, it would not be profitable to reduce price; therefore, policy of price increase would be appropriate (e.g., increase in price of cigarette, salt, petrol, and peak season air ticket does not affect demand). Conversely, if the demand is elastic, policy of price reduction rather than price increase would be profitable (e.g., increase in price of chocolate bar, fast-moving consumer goods, automobiles, etc., influence the demand).

•• *Market skimming*: Generally suitable for products with short life cycle that are likely to face competition in the future and are associated with high price and low volume (e.g., jewelry, digital technology, and PlayStation).

•• *Premium pricing*: Sometimes, customer behavior does not follow the law of demand.

For example, a dearer product is often perceived as superior quality, and higher prices usually increase the snob appeal of the product. These are generally true for the branded, luxury, and exclusive products. Higher prices that increase consumer readiness to buy may sound uneconomical but may not be unrealistic (e.g., status products, first-class air travel, Cunard Cruise, and luxury hotel suite).

•• *Value pricing*: Price is based on consumer perception and response from companies to retain sales due to increased competition or other compelling reasons (e.g., value meal at fast-food restaurants—consumers feel great value for his/her money, and companies are compelled to offer such value product to retain market share).

•• *Psychological pricing*: It is closely linked with the value pricing and plays greatly with the consumer perception (e.g., product price USD 9.9 instead of USD 10).

•• *Target pricing*: A specified profit level is targeted to set the price of a product. It is mostly used by the public utility companies that make huge investment in electricity, gas distribution, and so on. It is also followed in automobile industry.

•• *Marginal cost pricing*: It is the cost of producing incremental (one extra or less) item. It allows flexibility and variable pricing structure. Price of the product covers manufacturing cost but not the overhead cost (e.g., hotels and airlines often resort to marginal pricing to fill the capacity to sustain or improve profitability).

•• *Penetration pricing*: It is the price set to penetrate the market, usually for launching products into a new market. It is usually set at a low price to secure market share (e.g., cable or satellite TV operators, home phone, cell phone, and retail store products).

•• *Cost plus margin*: Price is based on actual cost plus a markup. Sometimes, it may result in overpricing or underpricing.

•• *Contribution pricing*: It is the price that ensures coverage of variable cost and a contribution to the fixed cost. In principle, it is similar to marginal pricing.

•• *Absorption/full cost pricing*: Price is set to cover both fixed and variable costs in full cost pricing, while in absorption cost pricing, it is set to absorb part of the fixed cost of manufacturing.

•• *Transfer pricing*: It is the price at which transactions are made among the associated enterprises or from one part of the company to another.

•• *Tender pricing*: Choosing the best value tender price and carrying out the work accordingly. The contracts are usually awarded on the basis of tender price.

•• *Predatory pricing*: It is deliberate underpricing of products to prevent new entrants or coerce rivals to withdraw from the market. It is also called destroyer pricing (e.g., competition between Burger King and McDonald's, and PepsiCo and Coca-Cola).

•• *Price discrimination*: Different prices are charged in different markets for the same product or services (e.g., price of suburban train ticket differs at different times of the day for the same journey). It is found when each market is impenetrable and having different price elasticity of demand. [1]

Oil pricing is markedly different from product pricing in conventional industry, which operates under the framework of deterministic input and assured output. But E&P industry operates under uncertainty wherein realization of investment is uncertain and may prove futile. Even if the discovery is made, it usually takes a long time to develop the field, assess commercial viability of reserves, and commence production. Because of uncertainty involved in

---

[1]Sanjib Chowdhury: Optimization and Business Improvement Studies in Upstream Oil and Gas Industry. John Wiley & Sons, Inc. 2016. P 287:289

the final outcome of investment, oil pricing is a complex, tricky, and challenging affair.

Oil price is greatly influenced by demand for oil, its supply and reserves position, future government policies on exploration and production, royalty and duties, various taxes and levies, and so on. In addition, other factors such as future technological and economic conditions, timing of production, revision of reserves, and so on, influence the pricing of oil.

Discovery of oil is the prime objective of exploration efforts. But it may so happen that instead of oil, only gas is discovered. Even with the production of oil, associated gas is produced. Therefore, it is a complex issue to calculate the cost of production of oil and that of gas separately. However, for simplification the production of oil and gas may be expressed in terms of "oil and oil equivalent gas" based on the heat content equivalence of oil and gas, which are as follows:

$1000 m^3$ (MSCM) of gas = 0.90 ton of oil equivalent or 1000 ft^3 (MSCF) of gas = 0.1767 barrel of oil equivalent

Oil price influences the economic development of a country—both developing and developed nations alike. In order to draw future plan of a country or industry or enterprise, it is necessary to project future demand for oil and more importantly oil price. But reliable forecast of oil price is elusive; it is an enigmatic issue and no long-term prediction has proved to be infallible; it provides at best a trend. There are various groups and agencies engaged in this task all over the world, as every nation has a stake in it. A large number of studies on oil price forecast and demand for oil have been made by various groups and agencies. Some of the notable groups and agencies whose predictions are somewhat reliable and are often referred to by many are International Energy Agency (IEA), US Energy Information Administration (EIA), PIRA Energy Group, Purvin & Gertz, Wood Mackenzie, Cambridge Energy Research Associates (CERA), Energy Security Analysis Inc. (ESAI), and others. [1]

The oil price moves in unpredictable cycle, and so do costs though these are correlated with price movements. Historically, periods of increasing oil prices result in tightening of fiscal terms (especially where the fiscal regime is not explicitly linked to oil price). The reaction to falling oil prices, however, tends to be slower and more erratic. On the upswing, governments are eager to capture a windfall; on the downswing, they are short of money and find cutting taxes unaffordable.

---

[1] Sanjib Chowdhury: Optimization and Business Improvement Studies in Upstream Oil and Gas Industry. John Wiley & Sons, Inc. 2016. P 289:290

As oil prices recovered from their low levels in the 1990s and increased in the first eight years of the twenty-first century, several countries introduced tougher fiscal measures. In the UK, the Government imposed a 10 per cent supplementary charge in 2002, then doubled it in 2005. In the US (Alaska), allowances were removed from certain fields in 2005 and new progressive taxes introduced, resulting in three large tax increases within three years. Venezuela increased royalty for new fields under its 2002 hydrocarbon law and removed royalty incentives for heavy oil in 2004, then increased royalty rates in 2006.

The Venezuela government went even further and introduced a compulsory transfer of equity from IOCs to PDVSA ensuring a minimum 50 per cent share for the national oil company. This was contested by some of the IOCs who remain in dispute with the government for appropriate compensation. Similarly, Bolivia increased royalty from 18 per cent to 50 per cent in 2005 while Ecuador introduced a 60 per cent windfall tax in 2006.

Following the oil price crash in 1986, many governments responded by reducing or even abolishing royalty rates and other 'regressive' fiscal terms in an

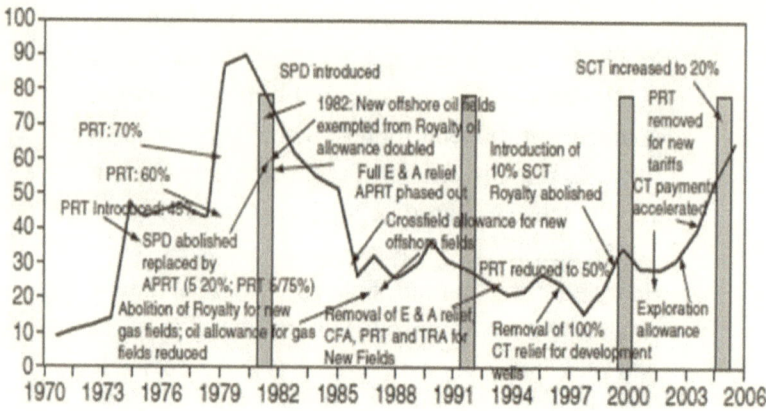

attempt to make the level of fiscal take more sensitive to project profitability than to revenues. But it can take many years for a country to reverse fiscal policies in order to attract new investment. After the oil price slump of 1998–1999, it took producing governments three to five years to implement new incentives for foreign oil investment. In Algeria, it took five years from the oil price collapse for a consensus to emerge on the need for reforms to the petroleum law, but by the time the changes came into effect in 2005, the oil price had rebounded to such an extent that the government reverted to more aggressive terms within a year.
(1)

---

(1)Philip Daniel, Michael Keen and Charles McPherson: The Taxation of Petroleum and Minerals. international Monetary Fund. 2010. P 109: 110

1.8. OIL PRICE HISTORY

Crude oil prices have seen wide price swings over the past decade whether it is due to apparent shortage or oversupply. At the time of writing, prices are close to $80 barrel which makes the so-called average price of approximately $21 per barrel (a number per barrel placed on the table by some economists) seems meaningless. Just as the determination of the so-called average structure is meaningless, so is an average price per barrel of oil. Even when adjusted for inflation to current dollars, an average price per barrel bears little relationship to reality, especially when reality is a much higher price per barrel. The analogy often used is that of a scientist or engineer standing with their left foot in a pail of boiling water and their right foot in a pail of ice water and declaring that they are comfortable because is at average temperature!

The very long-term view of petroleum pricing can be considered in the same way. Average prices, even when adjusted for inflation, do not help the consumer who has to bear the brunt of the price increases.

Historically (or, some might say, hysterically), crude oil prices varied from $2.50 to $3.00 from 1948 through the end of the 1960s. The price rose from $2.50 in 1948 to about $3.00 in 1957. From 1958 to 1970 prices were stable at about $3.00 per barrel.

Organization of Petroleum Exporting Countries (OPEC) was formed in 1960 with five founding members Iran, Iraq, Kuwait, Saudi Arabia, and Venezuela. By the end of 1971, six other nations (namely Qatar, Indonesia, Libya, United Arab Emirates, Algeria, and Nigeria) had swelled the membership ranks of OPEC.

Throughout this period, the petroleum exporting countries found increasing demand for their crude oil. In 1972, the price of crude oil was about $3.00 per barrel and by the end of 1974 the price of oil had quadrupled to over $12.00. The Yom Kippur War started with an attack on Israel by Syria and Egypt on October 5, 1973. Many countries in the western world showed strong support for Israel and, as a result, several of the Middle Eastern oil exporting nations imposed an embargo on those countries by decreasing oil.

From 1974 to 1978, the price of crude oil was relatively flat ranging from $12.21 per barrel to $13.55 per barrel. When adjusted for inflation the price over that period of time exhibited a moderate decline. Then events in Iran and Iraq (the overthrow of the Shah of Iran and the Iran–Iraq war) led to another round of crude oil price increases and crude oil prices rose to $35 per barrel in 1981.

The higher prices resulted in, among other actions usually involving energy conservation, increased exploration and production in the non-OPEC world. In mid-1985, oil prices were linked to the spot market for crude and by early 1986 (with increased production by some OPEC members), crude oil prices moved downward to $8 to $10 per barrel. The price of crude oil rose again in 1990 with the Iraqi invasion of Kuwait and the ensuing Gulf War, but following the war, crude oil prices entered a steady decline. The price cycle then turned up and from 1990 to 1997 world oil consumption increased by more than six million barrels per day.

The price increases came to a rapid end when, due to the downward trend in several Asian economies, higher OPEC production went downward.

A low point was reached in January 1999 after increased oil production from Iraq coincided with the Asian financial crisis, which reduced demand. The prices then rapidly increased, more than doubling by September 2000, then fell until the end of 2001 before steadily increasing, reaching $40 to $50 per barrel by September 2004. In October 2004, the price of crude oil exceeded $53 per barrel and for December delivery exceeded $55 per barrel. Crude oil prices surged to a record high above $60 a barrel in June 2005, sustaining a rally built on strong demand for gasoline and diesel and on concerns about refiners' ability to keep up. This trend continued into early August 2005 as crude oil prices surged past $65 per barrel. [1]

1.9. FUTURE OF OIL

The Hubbert theory assumes that oil reserves will not be replenished (i.e., that abiogenic replenishment is negligible) and predicts that future world oil production must inevitably reach a peak and then decline as these reserves are exhausted. Controversy surrounds the theory since as predictions for the time of the global peak is dependent on past production and discovery data used in the calculation.

For the United States, the prediction turned out to be correct and, after U.S. oil production peaked in 1971, it lost its excess production capacity, OPEC was able to manipulate oil prices.

Since then oil production in several other countries has also peaked. However, for a variety of reasons, it is difficult to predict the oil peak in any given region. Based on available production data, proponents have previously (and incorrectly) predicted the peak for the world to be in 1989, 1995, or in the 1995 to 2000 period. Other predictions have chosen 2007 and beyond for the peak of oil production. [2]

---

[1] James G. Speight: The Chemistry and Technology of Petroleum. FOURTH EDITION. Taylor & Francis Group, LLC. 2007. P 61:62

1.10. How Prices Reacted to the Shale Revolution

An overabundant supply, a demand weakened by sluggish economic activity and a lack of export infrastructure (pipelines, storage points and other logistic facilities) led to a strong reduction in natural gas prices in the US, which fell to 3 dollars per million British Thermal Units (MMBTU) in 2012 from 9 in 2008. By contrast, in Europe, where prices were still linked to oil quotations, the cost of gas remained high, resulting in an increasing differential (soared to 8 dollars per MMBTU in 2012 from 1.1 in 2007) which penalized European countries (IEA 2012a). Similarly, the growing production of LTO explains part of the negative price differential between WTI and Brent, the benchmark crudes for the US and EU markets respectively, which has endured since the end of 2010. Despite this evidence, it would be unwise to simply deduce that the increased supply accruing from SF production will exercise a downward pressure on prices: unconventional upstream activities are economically viable when market prices are high enough to generate cash flows that cover the higher extraction costs. The IEA estimates that oil prices must remain above 60–80 dollars per barrel for LTO to be profitably exploited, which is three to four times

([2])James G. Speight: The Chemistry and Technology of Petroleum. FOURTH EDITION. Taylor & Francis Group, LLC. 2007. P 62

the break-even price estimated for extraction using standard techniques. An analogous evaluation places the break-even point for SG at around 5 dollars per MMBTU, somewhat lower when Natural Gas Liquids (NGL), a by-product whose price is anchored to the oil price, is jointly extracted. In fact, the number of active wells decreased substantially in 2012, when the price of Henry Hub (HH), the US gas market benchmark, plummeted to a historical low of 2 dollars per MMBTU, considerably below the break-even price. [1]

   Logistic costs also affect the competitiveness of SFs. For instance, SG can only be exported as Liquefied Natural Gas (LNG), but on top of transport costs this requires a costly regasification process that entails a 30 % loss of the energy content. Cheniere Energy, which is running the most important project for exporting LNG from the United States, has signed contracts with several Asian countries linking the LNG price to the HH and waiving the standard "take or pay" clause. This company estimates that these buyers would pay a price for LNG of around 11–12 dollars per MMBTU if the HH price stays in the region of 4–5 dollars per MMBTU. This is still lower than the 15–17 dollars currently paid by Japan for its LNG imports, although it is somewhat higher than the

[1]Rossella Bardazzi • Maria Grazia Pazienza Alberto Tonini: European Energy and Climate Security. Springer International Publishing Switzerland 2016. P 138

average price prevailing over 2011–2013 in Europe (10.8 dollars per MMBTU).

Finally, the abundant supply of SG may have indirectly affected other international energy markets, e.g. the replacement of coal with cheaper natural gas in US power generation has increased the volume of US coal available for export. This fact may explain why, starting from 2012, the market price of coal, normally linked to oil prices, has been falling. From a global perspective, the relevance of SFs to world supply should increase world average extraction costs, with possible repercussions over the medium term on international market prices. [1]

The '2012 World Energy Council Survey of Energy Resources: Shale Gas – What's New' predicted that shale gas development would have a "significant impact on the dynamics and prices" of future natural gas markets. This latest study explores the implications of the rapid growth in unconventional gas supplies on global markets and concludes that, unconventional gas has become a global phenomenon and will continue to have global implications for some time to come. The weight of these changes on the global supply landscape is an important consideration

---

[1] Rossella Bardazzi • Maria Grazia Pazienza Alberto Tonini: European Energy and Climate Security. Springer International Publishing Switzerland 2016. P 139

for energy professionals seeking to understand the future of the industry. [1]

The speed at which unconventional natural gas has disrupted markets is best evidenced in North America, led by the US, where a regional supply glut drove investments that turned import terminals to export terminals, power stations from coal to gas, and drove substantial E&P activity. In 2014, US shale gas production represented 47% of total US natural gas production and more than 10% of global natural gas production. In 2016, the influence of shale gas is stronger than ever, as it enters European and Asian markets in the form of LNG.

The US Energy Information Administration (EIA) expects the US to become a net exporter of natural gas by 2017.3 According to company announcements and the Federal Energy Regulatory Commission (FERC), there are five US LNG export projects under construction, reflecting 62.7 million tons per annum (mtpa) of new US LNG export capacity coming online through 2019.

When these projects are completed, North America will become the fourth-largest LNG export region, behind Asia Pacific, the Middle East, and Africa as evidenced in Figure

---

[1] World Energy Resources. World Energy Council. 2016. P 4

2. The US alone will account for almost one-fifth of global liquefaction capacity and will become the third-largest LNG export capacity holder in the world, after Qatar (77.0 mtpa) and Australia (86.5 mtpa).5 Significant impact to natural gas hubs globally will accompany this rapid change in the North America landscape. [1]

Increased supply of natural gas from shale resources and the associated liquids contributes to lower prices for natural gas and hydrocarbon gas liquids (HGL), which support higher levels of industrial output. The energy-intensive bulk chemicals industry benefits from lower prices for fuel (primarily natural gas) and feedstocks (natural gas and HGL), as consumption of natural gas and HGL feedstocks increases by more than 50% from 2013 to 2040 in the Reference case, mostly as a result of growth in the total capacity of U.S. methanol, ammonia (mostly for nitrogenous fertilizers), and ethylene catalytic crackers. Increased availability of HGL leads to much slower growth in the use of heavy petroleum-based naphtha feedstocks compared to the lighter HGL feedstocks (ethane, propane, and butane). With sustained low HGL prices, the feedstock slate continues to favor HGL at unprecedented levels. [2]

---

[1] World Energy Resources. World Energy Council. 2016. P 14
[2] U.S. Energy Information Administration. Annual Energy Outlook 2015. P 6

When OPEC unexpectedly caused the price of oil to jump from under $10 a barrel to over $30 in 1973, the United States government thought it prudent to invest in methods to recover oil from shale. The economics of such a project were so costly, and its chances of success so remote, that no private company could afford to undertake it. It was clearly a case where subsidies from the government were justified by the potential usefulness to society of a successful outcome.

The oil in shale is contained in a substance called kerogen which is tightly bound to the rock. This rock can be excavated and then processed above ground. Or, if shale is close to the surface, it can be strip mined by first removing the topsoil to expose the rock and then using heavy machinery to excavate the shale. [1]

Things change quickly in this industry. In Chicago they say 'If you don't like the weather, give it a few hours' and this saying applies to the oil markets and the growing fascination with shale oil. Things changed relatively quickly as crude oil production doubled from 5mm b/d in 2011 to 9.5mm b/d in 2015.

---

[1] Sidney Borowitz: FAREWELL FOSSIL FUELS Reviewing America's. Energy Policy. Plenum Press, New York in 1999. P 60

Demand for crude that runs through US refineries jumped from 15mm b/d in 2013 to tip the scales at a peak of 17mm b/d this year. If for anything, the truth is that crude oil production in the US is at record highs and consumption of that crude is also at record highs.

In the eight months that have passed in 2015, the year started with major concerns about the viability of shale crude production. As oil prices were tumbling under $60, talk in the market was that break even for shale producers was at best $50.

Recently several producers have said that in some areas they have seen break even falling to $20 in some regions. An overall estimate of where this break-even number is on average, most are thinking it's closer to $35 than it is $50.

A lot of factors have combined and have contributed to change the thinking about these break evens this year, in addition to cost restructuring making a major impact. There has been the reduction of labor and a lot of overspend in those areas. There has been a restructuring of cost of land on which production is being completed. There has also been an emergence of 'walking rigs' and more efficient oil recovery from a single site bring costs down. Additionally, technology has been upfront and making an impact.

Technology has now helped frack producers pull more crude from a single drill site. There is a difference in materials being used, different angles of equipment and multiple frack positions within a first frack. Data mining has become as material as the frack mining. Within milliseconds of a producing well, we are getting data that is not just catching real time inefficiencies; it's positioning the site for a major return on the longer-term efficiency. As technology continues to advance, the break even for the shale oil plays are lowering. As the breakeven levels have lowered, the American oil industry is now facing a 'new normal'. It has now become the swing producer in the world. If OPEC is waiting for the US to pull back production, the US may not see any relief soon from lower prices. Oil has become as American of a commodity as corn. There will be no reason, outside of falling oil drilling economics, to see the industry weaken to the point that it is not maintaining more production than it needs to import.

There is still a risk that shale plays may falter. The industry is working hard to push the recovery of the US economy, but there has not been a positive year of GDP over 2%. If pressure continues to come from areas outside the US, the economy may get pushed back into a weaker recovery. If that causes demand to fade, this is when the crude oil production will find its weakness. Production cannot be expected to stay above 9mm b/d if refinery demand slides to under 16mm b/d on a consistent basis.

There is another risk to the US producer that lies on the fringe; the cost of imports compared to the US crude. The basic spread between the US crude benchmark and the foreign benchmark has seen a brief period of parity this past year, but if it is averaged out since 2011, there is a difference that has favored the Brent by about $15. This is based on if the cost of foreign crude tumbles to a discount on a consistent basis.

In regards to the US storage market, there is only good news ahead. The US continues to produce oil, but it is still far from all the oil that is used on a daily basis. More than 7mm b/d of foreign crude is still imported and before there is any decline in US production, that number will have to see a reduction.

The recent deal with Mexico and the US to 'swap' crude barrels is a step in the right direction, but more importantly, a sign that the US government is thinking about this situation. There will not be a drop in US crude oil production as long as the only alternative to meet demand is to import crude oil.

Crude in America is a benchmark that is based on storage; West Texas Intermediate (WTI) crude. This grade of WTI is priced on a financial market that delivers to storage in

Cushing, Oklahoma. However, since the growth of shale oil production in America though, there has been a shift of focus away from this terminal site. This is because there is a large amount of crude that is now produced in Texas and is delivered into the Gulf Coast refineries.

Along with this, more people are now developing more storage in the US Gulf to accommodate more crude that is being delivered to other refineries in America. Economics have already come together to ship US crude to Canada from the US Gulf.

In the North Dakota region where the first of the shale boom was seen, barrels are being pulled from that region on rail and over to refineries in the Midwest and on to the east coast. Additionally, a lot of crude has moved down to the Cushing area when the production first started to rise, but as the price of US crude has maintained a healthy discount to foreign crude, moving crude from North Dakota to the east coast has become more attractive.

This is leaving the current benchmark in a state of ineffectiveness but it is also creating more opportunity for people to explore other areas to increase storage capacity and terminal sites.

Granted, this easing with the falling price of crude once again, but as recently as earlier this year, the commodity that was hottest in the marketplace was storage and terminal space.

With the increase of crude production and even more so, refined product exports – storage and terminal space is at a premium. All markets have their ebb and flow, but as the low cost of oil continues, it is to the advantage of US producers to meet the refiners' demands and for refiners to meet consumers growing demand.

The spread of the US benchmark WTI to the foreign benchmark of Brent, continues to see the American crude at an advantage. This advantage supports the US as the premier area to see more product produced and exported at a lower price to the consumer. Moving ahead, more storage tanks and terminals are needed to deal with current production, but also to deal with what seems to be an inevitable move to export crude oil. Shale is here to stay and it is far from over. The increase of only 400K b/d of domestic production from January 1 to the current levels marks the smallest increase to production since it started climbing in 2011. It is a better outlook for shale producers as the price of oil has dipped from $60 to $40.

However, things change quickly and if a way back to the upside is found, more oil is not going to be enough. [1]

---

[1] Carl Larry: The new normal for the US oil industry.

Recent surge in the supply of unconventional gas, mostly shale gas, is reshaping the energy landscapes of gas-rich countries, revitalizing their economies, and impacting long-term geopolitical interests around the world. Called *"Shale Revolution,"* it is substantially altering the US energy mix (increasing gas share to 32 % at the expense of coal that dropped to 34 %, in 2012), reducing dependence on oil imports (from 60 to 42 %) and reducing GHG emissions (1.7 % in 2011). It is also spurring manufacturing in downstream industries: petrochemical, chemical, metallurgical, and other energy-intensive industries. At the same time, low gas prices are impacting the economics of renewables (wind and solar) and, especially, nuclear. But there are also cautious attitudes, e.g., are the gas resources substantial enough to warrant serious investments in converting transport from gasoline to gas for fleets and private vehicles? How availability of relatively cheap gas will affect the prospects of carbon sequestration technology, and, in the long term, carbon mitigation policies?

These questions will need to be answered as part of the energy policy adjustments to the new energy landscape.

Tank storage magazine. Volume 1, Issue 1.2015.

Shale gas boom in the USA is having impact not only on renewables and nuclear sectors, but, quite surprisingly (and unexpectedly), it is promoting coal usage by European utilities, despite the EU's environmental policies dedicated to curbing the share of coal in their energy mix (the EU environmental policy calls for a 20 % reduction in carbon emissions from 1990 levels by 2020 via growing role of renewables in electricity generation). While North America's surge in shale gas production pushed down NG prices to decade's lows, prompting power plants to switch from coal to gas, unwanted at home American coal has increasingly found its way to European markets, where it displaced more expensive gas. This trend shows how disruptive could shale gas become for traditional industries such as power generation, leading to unforeseen (and often even perverse) outcomes across the global energy system. The US coal exports to Europe increased by 29 % in 2012 (against the backdrop of a reduced Chinese demand), dropping European coal prices from $130 per ton in March 2011 down to $86 per ton in February 2013.

This trend was exacerbated by a sharp fall in the price of carbon allowances under the EU's flagship Emission Trading System (ETS) and rising European prices for NG. Prices for permits in the EU's ETS were at about €4 ($5.35) per metric ton in January 2013 (Note that in 2005, UN study estimated that penalties for emitting CO2 would have to be at least $25–$30 per metric ton to make it work.). As a result, gas-fired electricity output in Germany fell 16 % in 2012, while coal-fired plants added output by the same amount. In the EU, in 2011, gas-fired generation fell by 17 % and coal-fired generation increased by 11 %. Despite the recent increase in coal usage in Europe, many experts believe that this trend is short-lived and temporary and is just a matter of the economics of the current energy market.

IEA projects that the trend of European demand for coal is close to peaking, and by 2017 it will drop to levels close to those in 2011.

Besides economical, there are quite serious geopolitical ramifications of the Shale Revolution. For example, because the USA can now sell gas at 75 % below what Russian Gazprom charges East European customers, Gazprom has been forced to lower gas prices sold to Europe, and it is being investigated by the European Commission for price fixing. Because of cheaper gas prices, the Gazprom's market value in 2012 dropped threefold compared to 2008, and some gas projects in the Arctic have been canceled. Analysts now question the Gazprom's future as Russia's veritable cash cow. [1]

---

[1] Nazim Muradov: Liberating Energy from Carbon: Introduction to Decarbonization. Springer

2. Supply and demand

Cheap imported oil replaced coal, and although this was a period of marked advances in European co-operation this was not reflected in the oil and gas sector.

The different energy sources came under a number of separate national authorities and Community institutions, and each member country had its own set of enactments and regulations, particularly regarding pricing, commercial policy, taxation and investment. Throughout the 1960s and the 1970s, the European Communities were working hard to create a Common Market with common rules applying to the main fields of economic policy, but because of government resistance and oil company unwillingness the energy sector was not among these fields and remained "a pocket of resistance to integration". Even though numerous policy proposals were made by the Commission or its predecessor, these proposals came to nothing with member states variously rejecting or ignoring them. [1]

Due to its rising energy demand, China has had to import large quantities of oil to meet its domestic demand. Despite being a net

---

Science+Business Media New York 2014. P 15: 16

[1]Rossella Bardazzi • Maria Grazia Pazienza Alberto Tonini: European Energy and Climate Security. Springer International Publishing Switzerland 2016. P 15

exporter of petroleum in 1990, China's import share of petroleum dramatically increased from less than 8% in 1995 to approximately 50% in 2006. By 2007, China's imports of crude oil and products reached 184 million tons, becoming the third largest importer after USA and Japan (BP 2008). [1]

There are many factors that require China to import more petroleum products. Of them, household car ownership is one of the most important. Private car purchases have increased rapidly. In 2000 there were only 0.5 cars per hundred urban households. By 2006 it had risen to 4.32 cars per hundred urban households. The rise in electricity consumption has been driven not only by rapidly growing Industrial demand, but also an even more rapidly spreading ownership of household appliances. For example, household air conditioners and microwave ovens trebled over 2003–2009, from 30 and 17 to 88 and 51 per hundred urban households, respectively. As a result, household electricity consumption has expanded rapidly. Household electricity consumption was 48 billion kWh in 1990, doubling to 101 billion kWh in 1995 and doubling again to 201 billion kWh by 2002. In 2006 this figure had risen to nearly 325 billion kWh. As a consequence, there has been a growing shortage of electricity in

---

[1]Hengyun Ma 1 Les Oxley: China's Energy Economy. Springer-Verlag Berlin Heidelberg 2012. P 3

China which has attracted growing interest and concern. [1]

In fact, with the high growth rate of energy demand, China is presently faced with two major energy-related issues, namely the shortage of domestic petroleum resources (e.g., accounting for more than half imports) and environmental pollution associated with its coal resource (e.g., accounting for 70% of primary energy supply). Therefore, reducing the energy intensity and increasing the share of renewable energy are two of the most important priorities for China to undertake in order to realize its energy and environment goals in the new Millennium. [2]

In general, China's energy imports are quite limited. Until 1996 China was a net exporter in terms of aggregate energy. Post-1996, China's aggregate energy imports increased, but with no obvious trend. Only in recent years has a discernable, stable increase in net energy imports emerged, rising from 53 million tons standard coal equivalence in 2000, to over 200 million tons standard coal equivalence in 2006. This means China's energy import dependence has increased from 3.8% in 2000 to 8.2% in 2006. This pattern of energy

---

[1] Hengyun Ma l Les Oxley: China's Energy Economy. Springer-Verlag Berlin Heidelberg 2012. P 3
[2] Hengyun Ma l Les Oxley: China's Energy Economy. Springer-Verlag Berlin Heidelberg 2012. P 51

trade is determined by two major characteristics of China's energy supply and demand; an abundance of coal deposits and rising demand for petroleum. [1]

Strong economic development leads to increase in the industrial sector's demand for energy. The industrial sector consumes at least 37 % of the total energy supply, which is relatively more energy intensive than any other major sectors including household, agriculture, and public services. A recent study conducted by the US Environmental Protection Agency (EPA) in 2007 revealed that 30 % of the energy consumed by the industrial and commercial premises is wasted due to inefficient way of using, and lack of risk management tools.

Energy use efficiency is an important issue, due to limits in replacing energy as an input factor by other possible substitutable factors in the production process. Efficient use of energy may reduce the amount of fuel or primary energy needed to produce energy output such as electricity. Efficient use of energy will reduce the energy intensity, which may lead to reduction in the corresponding global emissions of air pollution and greenhouse gases. A key variable of interest in a study of efficiency and productivity in the industrial sector is the energy demand. It can be considered as a significant

---

[1] Hengyun Ma 1 Les Oxley: China's Energy Economy. Springer-Verlag Berlin Heidelberg 2012. P 73

variable in the cost structure of any industry, and an essential determinant of the level of energy demand. This book is concerned with determining the following measures: [1]

1. The overall energy demand at the industrial sector.

2. The rate of technical change that causes shifts in the energy demand over time.

3. The variance of energy demand and its determinants.

4. The efficiency in the use of energy, given production output and industrial sector's characteristics

Any increase in the demand for energy will lead to a corresponding increase in its price. According to EIA (2011), the crude oil price will average 100 USD per barrel for the next 20 years, it will reach more than 200 USD per barrel in 2030. This increase in the energy price according to the report is due to increase in the demand for oil and the production cost. Industrial policy decision makers need to understand the importance of the energy in the industrial production structure, in order to assess and formulate necessary measures of energy conservation. Accordingly, it is important to acquire knowledge about the energy demand and

---

[1] Nabaz T. Khayyat: Energy Demand in Industry. Springer Science+Business Media Dordrecht 2015. P 2

its characteristics such as the possible substitutability between energy and other input factors of production.

Unlike normal goods where supply response is used to meet increase in demand, in the case of energy, the demand response of the market is employed to reduce increase in the demand. For example, the use of smart grid technology as part of demand response program allows for the application of price variation/discrimination by type of consumer, location, season, and hours of the day, with the aim to reduce energy consumption. Smart grid technology improves the producer's and consumer's ability to optimize generation and consumption of energy. A better optimization improves energy use and efficiency, which will also reduce the amount of energy generated by peak time reserve capacity at high cost, and also reduces energy consumption during peak time at high price. [1]

Regardless of all the challenges and uncertainties, OPEC Member Countries continue to invest in additional upstream capacities. On top of the huge capacity maintenance costs that Member Countries are faced with, they continue to invest in new projects and reinforce their commitment to the oil and gas market as well as to the security of supply for all consumers.

---

[1] Nabaz T. Khayyat: Energy Demand in Industry. Springer Science+Business Media Dordrecht 2015. P 3: 4

Needless to say, this is only a reflection of OPEC's well-known policy that is clearly stated in its Long-Term Strategy and its Statute. In the medium-term, about 160 projects, with an overall estimated cost of some $156 billion, are being undertaken by OPEC Member Countries. [1]

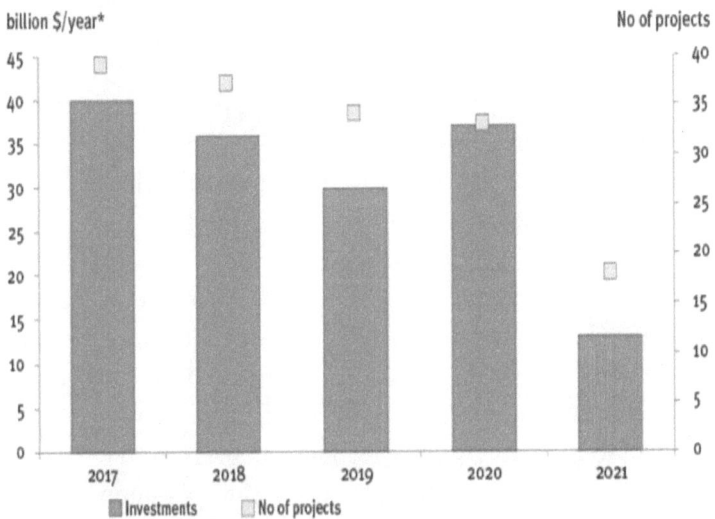

2.1. Oil demand

In recent years, along with the rapid development of the Chinese economy, the international oil price has climbed substantially. The demand for oil reached a record high, so that a common refrain was "the higher the price

[1] http://www.opec.org/opec_web/en/index.htm

of oil, the greater the demand of oil." There was even the belief that the rise in oil prices had no impact on energy savings. There are many factors affecting oil demand, such as economic development and, in particular, oil prices. Therefore, it is especially important to research the effects of the oil price on oil demand in terms of scientifically understanding the functions of the price mechanisms and the effects of changing prices on energy savings.

Oil price is the main factor that influences oil consumption and production. We cannot ignore the fact that a rise in oil prices reflects a supply shortage in the markets for crude oil and refined oil products, along with an increasing demand for oil. the OECD members will need to import two-thirds of their total oil demand by 2030, from 50 % today. It is no doubt that the rapid increase in oil demand will lead to a relatively slow response in terms of the oil price and that the demand of transportation will take up a rising share of the total oil consumption. However, compared with other energy-consumption sectors, there is essentially no elasticity between the transportation demand and oil prices, so the response of oil demand to international crude oil price variations is becoming slower and smaller. At the same time, rising demand and changes in the costs of production will affect the oil price directly, and people generally believe that oil prices will rise in the future; that is, $87/barrel in 2015 and

$115/barrel in 2030. It is also believed that the marginal cost of supplies will increase and that the oil demand of non-OECD members will also rise, which will influence the oil price and cause it to rise. Therefore, the oil price and the oil demand affect each other, and the price elasticity influences the oil demand. Further, the research on price elasticity becomes more significant. [1]

We believe that oil price changes in the year, including the processes of change, are bound to affect the demand for crude oil and that using the monthly price of crude oil may be more appropriate in calculating the price elasticity of oil demand in China. Crude oil is the energy source that is the pillar of economic development, so uneven economic development will greatly affect the demand for crude oil. At the same time, international political factors, as well as international speculators and investment funds, will exacerbate the variation in oil prices throughout a given year. the monthly average price of Brent crude oil in 2008 was $96.85/barrel, where the highest price was $132.72/barrel and the lowest price was $39.95/barrel, or a spread of $92.77/barrel. Thus, using annual data to calculate the elasticity of demand for crude oil will lead to considerable error. On the other hand, China's coal energy represented a large proportion of the energy

[1]Yi-Ming Wei • Hua Liao: Energy Economics: Energy Efficiency in China. Springer International Publishing Switzerland 2016. P 234

supply (68.7 % in 2008), so it is very important to estimate the alternative price elasticity of coal to crude oil. Moreover, coal is affected by seasonal effects (e.g., winter heating in northern China is mainly by coal). Therefore, it is necessary to use monthly data to calculate the elasticity of the substitution of coal for crude oil. [1]

The demand for crude oil is influenced by many factors. From our perspective, industrial production accounts for most of the demand and the use of GDP is the preferred income variable. However, no GDP monthly data is currently available for China and, as mentioned above, using monthly data is better for determining the crude oil demand price elasticity. Hence, we use monthly industrial gross output to represent variations in income and crude oil demand because industry is one of the main oil-consuming sectors and it represents most of the crude oil demand. Moreover, the inventory of crude oil and the industrial production process can influence oil demand as well, so we use the industrial products price index (PPI), which measures the changes in the prices of various commodities at different stages of production. Other factors, like weather, can also affect oil demand. During cold weather, people need heat, so there is an increase in oil

---

[1] Yi-Ming Wei • Hua Liao: Energy Economics: Energy Efficiency in China. Springer International Publishing Switzerland 2016. P 234

demand. Therefore, the monthly demand for crude oil includes a monthly adjustment to account for cyclical factors such as seasonal changes that affect the computation of the actual crude oil demand price elasticity. [1]

We believe that oil demand is mainly affected by domestic industrial production and that the international oil price has little effect on oil demand, creating the slogan "the higher the international oil price, the greater the imports of oil." In the meantime, oil imports in China play a big part in terms of spot goods, whose prices are the average price during arrival and departure at a particular port. Thus, international investors always drive-up prices during this period, leading to higher oil prices on the spot market than in ordinary markets. On the other hand, China's external dependence on oil is extremely high (already over 51 %), so oil demand in the short term is very high. Moreover, the Chinese people expect rising prices due to both rapid development in recent years and the overall rise in international oil prices. [2]

To cope with the huge growth in demand, the private oil companies decided to organize their operations on a more elastic basis

---

[1] Yi-Ming Wei • Hua Liao: Energy Economics: Energy Efficiency in China. Springer International Publishing Switzerland 2016. P 235
[2] Yi-Ming Wei • Hua Liao: Energy Economics: Energy Efficiency in China. Springer International Publishing Switzerland 2016. P 243

by diversifying the areas in which they were prospecting and by stepping up production. After World War II, the rapid development of the oil market in Western Europe was complementary to the success of the oil companies in finding new oil fields, notably in the Middle East, under what were exceptionally favorable conditions. Although differently placed one from the other, the seven major companies all had important Middle East oil interests in which the royalty and price structure operated in such a way as to give the companies a comfortable share of the economic rents. In these circumstances, with the oil companies enjoying a high after-tax income and therefore a high cash flow from their upstream operations, it came to seem natural to them to develop the Western European market as a complementary activity which disposed of their oil through refining and market activities, often conducted on a break-even basis or even at a loss. Action by the United States government in the form of import quotas to protect its home production caused the bulk of the increased supply to be directed to Europe. [1]

In 2015, the price of Brent stood at $52/barrel, down nearly 47% compared to 2014 ($99/barrel). The very perturbed geopolitical situation had little influence, apart from the

---

[1] Rossella Bardazzi • Maria Grazia Pazienza Alberto Tonini: European Energy and Climate Security. Springer International Publishing Switzerland 2016. P 15

concerns at the start of the year (26 March) following the armed intervention in Yemen by Saudi Arabia and its allies.

Overall, the excess of supply determined the price, which fell to below $50 after August, falling to $38 in December and to below $30 at the start of 2016. The continuation of OPEC's policy to defend its market share and the slight decrease in US production are the reasons for this downward price pressure. Based on future markets, since August 2015 the expected price for 2016 has fluctuated between $30 and $60/b. [1]

---

[1] Investments in exploration/production and refining 2015. IFP Energies Nouvelles - January 2016. P 7

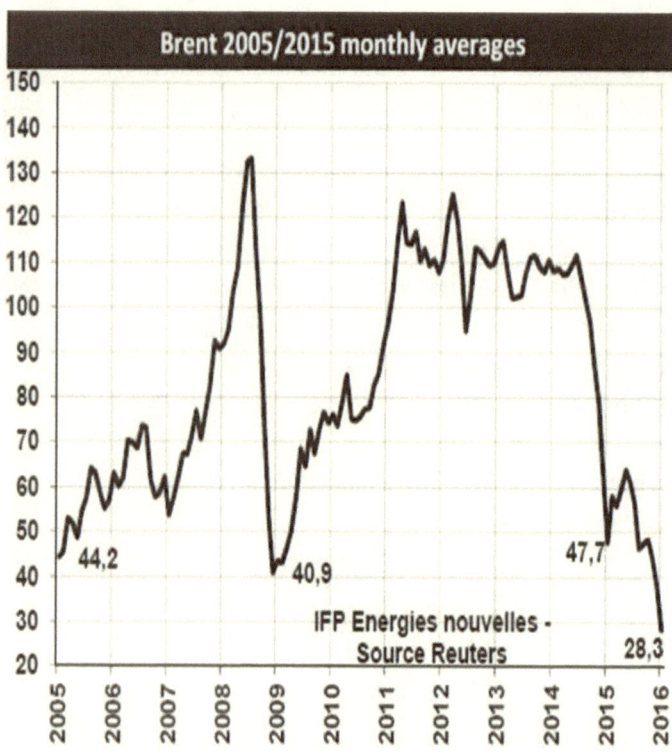

The main factors influencing the price will be: the level of global growth, which, according to the IMF, will possibly be "disappointing and uneven"; Iranian exports, likely to increase by about 0.5 Mb/d in the short term; the drop in US production caused by the decrease in drilling activity and, globally, the more gradual effects of the drop in upstream investments on production capacities; the change or otherwise in OPEC policy, which has been in effect since 2014; and the influence on production of growing regional tensions in the Middle East. [1]

World oil demand grew by around 1.0 million barrels per day (mb/d) in 2014, in line with initial projections back in July 2013. Lower oil prices and improvements in economic activity in major demand centers such as the US and India resulted in better-than-expected acceleration in oil demand in 4Q14.

OECD demand continued on its descending trend in 2014. OECD America is the only region with positive growth at 0.09 mb/d while OECD Europe and Asia Pacific declined by 0.18 mb/d each. Non- OECD regions, on the other hand, grew by 1.23 mb/d in 2014, with China accounting for the majority of growth, rising by 0.40 mb/d. The Middle East, Other Asia and Latin America grew by 0.25 mb/d, 0.21 mb/d and 0.20 mb/d, respectively. [1]

In OECD Americas, 2H14 improvements in macroeconomic indicators, supported by lower oil prices, boosted transportation fuel consumption in the US.

However, growth levels in other countries in the region — Mexico and Canada — modestly increased or declined. In the US, 2014 ended with positive oil demand growth for the second consecutive year, rising by around 0.5 per cent y-o-y. This is primarily the result of

---

[1]Investments in exploration/production and refining 2015. IFP Energies Nouvelles - January 2016. P 7
[1]Organization of the Petroleum Exporting Countries. Annual Report 2014. P 13

a rise in 2H14 affecting the overall figure for 2014, influenced by lower prices for transportation fuels gasoline, diesel oil and jet fuel. US oil demand in 1H14 shrank by around 20 trillion barrels per day (tb/d) y-o-y, despite additional requirements for heating purposes, as weather conditions were colder than initially anticipated in 1Q14. However, the poor performance of natural gas liquids (NGLs), residual fuels and gasoline in 2Q14 dragged overall average consumption growth lower, to its lowest point on a quarterly basis since 4Q12. [1]

In OECD Europe, 2014 oil demand generally contracted by around 0.2 mb/d, with the bulk of losses in 1H14 and some signs of improvement thereafter, as lower oil prices propelled oil consumption.

Overall oil demand in all of the four big consumers — Germany, UK, France and Italy — declined in 2014. Looking at the product mix, diesel demand remained weak, mainly as temperatures recorded warmer readings from one year earlier, promoting lower consumption for heating purposes. Gasoline was flat y-o-y, despite steady vehicle sales growth figures for the last 18 consecutive months. The major reasons for this stagnation in gasoline growth included continued progress in efficiency standards, the use of alternative fuels in the

---

[1] Organization of the Petroleum Exporting Countries. Annual Report 2014. P 13: 14

transportation sector, high taxation polices in major European consumer countries and slower economic momentum than initially anticipated. (1)

In the Middle East, oil demand saw opposing trends in 2014. In Saudi Arabia, oil demand rose strongly again, growing by more than nine per cent yo-y, while geopolitical turbulence in some parts of the region implied sharp declines, for example in Iraqi and Syrian oil demand. (2)

	2011	2012	2013	1Q14	2Q14	3Q14	4Q14	2014
World demand (mb/d)								
OECD	46.4	45.9	46.1	45.7	45.0	46.0	46.6	45.8
OECD Americas	24.0	23.6	24.1	23.9	23.8	24.4	24.7	24.2
OECD Europe	14.3	13.8	13.7	13.0	13.6	13.9	13.5	13.5
OECD Asia Pacific	8.2	8.5	8.3	8.9	7.7	7.7	8.4	8.1
DCs	27.3	28.3	29.0	29.4	29.8	30.4	29.7	29.8
FSU	4.3	4.4	4.5	4.4	4.2	4.6	4.9	4.5
Other Europe	0.6	0.6	0.6	0.6	0.6	0.6	0.7	0.7
China	9.4	9.7	10.1	10.1	10.6	10.3	10.9	10.5
(a) Total world demand	88.1	89.0	90.3	90.2	90.2	92.0	92.8	91.3

The medium-term oil demand outlook for the period 2016–2022 shows an increase of 6.9 mb/d, rising from 95.4 mb/d to 102.3 mb/d. This corresponds to a healthy average annual increase of almost 1.2 mb/d. Demand in

---

(1)Organization of the Petroleum Exporting Countries. Annual Report 2014. P 14
(2)Organization of the Petroleum Exporting Countries. Annual Report 2014. P 16

Developing countries is expected to be strong, increasing from 43.2 mb/d in 2016 to 49.6 mb/d in 2022.

Globally, oil demand has been revised upwards by 2.24 mb/d in 2022 compared to the WOO 2016. This revision includes the upward shift to the baseline (+1.2 mb/d) in 2016. In addition, in this year's WOO, OECD regional oil demand is expected to grow until 2019, before the trend reverses. In last year's publication, OECD demand grew only until 2017. [1]

Long-term oil demand is expected to increase by 15.8 mb/d, rising from 95.4 mb/d in 2016 to 111.1 mb/d in 2040. Demand in the OECD region is anticipated to show a significant decline of 8.9 mb/d over the forecast period. Driven by an expanding middle class, high population growth rates and stronger economic growth potential, developing countries' oil demand is expected to increase by almost 24 mb/d. China is anticipated to continue to be the largest oil consumer over the forecast period, adding 6 mb/d to reach 17.8 mb/d by 2040. India will be the region with the second largest overall demand growth, adding 5.9 mb/d between 2016 and 2040. Indian demand growth is also set to witness the fastest average growth of 3.6% p.a.

Long term global oil demand growth is forecast to decelerate steadily, falling from an

---

[1] http://www.opec.org/opec_web/en/index.htm

annual average of around 1.3 mb/d during the period 2016–2020 to only 0.3 mb/d every year between 2035 and 2040. This deceleration is a result of slowing GDP growth, assumed oil price increases, a structural shift of economies towards a more service-oriented structure, efficiency improvements as a result of tightening energy efficiency policies and/or technological improvements, and oil facing strong competition from other energy sources. [1]

A year ago, prospects seemed dim that the lifting of the US crude oil export ban would become a reality with the Congress and President at odds on nearly every issue. However, in mid-December 2015, as part of the deal on tax and spending legislation, the ban on crude oil exports was lifted.

Prior to the lifting of the export ban, it was perfectly legal to export all the crude one wanted for use in Canada. According to the Energy Information Administration (EIA), exports to Canada grew from less than 50,000 barrels per day in 2011 to a peak of 524,000 barrels per day in May 2015. Alaskan North Slope crude oil could also be exported as long as it was transported on a Jones Act tanker.

Soon after the legislation was enacted, companies were racing to announce that they had exported crude oil to destinations other than

---

[1] http://www.opec.org/opec_web/en/index.htm

Canada. It was first reported that Vitol was loading a crude oil cargo out of the Enterprise Products Partners terminal in early January. On December 30, 2015, ConocoPhillips and NuStar said they had exported the first cargo of crude oil and it was loading out of Corpus Christi. During the next few months, reports of additional crude oil exports surfaced. Citgo reportedly sold a cargo to its parent company PDVSA, Trafigura had sold a cargo into Israel and ExxonMobil sold a cargo loading out of Beaumont Texas to an affiliated refinery in Italy. Cosmo Oil purchased a crude oil cargo for one of its refineries in Japan. At its fourth quarter 2015 earnings call on January 28, 2016, Enterprise Products CEO Jim Teague said that they had nominations to move six million barrels of crude oil.

The problem of disposing a North American light sweet crude oil surplus for a refining system built to handle heavy sour crude oil had been solved. The only thing left to do was ensure that enough pipeline, storage and dock logistics were available along with favorable arbitrage economics to keep the export flow going.

Due to its proximity to the Eagle Ford Shale, the Port of Corpus Christi has greatly benefitted from shipments of crude oil to water. Pipelines owned by Nustar, Energy Transfer Partners, Kinder Morgan, Magellan, Enterprise and Plains can deliver vast amounts of production to area terminals for subsequent loading. This of course includes not only exports, but shipments via Jones Act Tankers and barges to other ports in the United States including Houston, St James, Philadelphia and even Los Angeles.

It is estimated that there is at least 1.4 million barrels per day of inbound pipeline capacity available to deliver into 11 million barrels of terminal storage. According to its website, the port loaded nearly 30 million tons or about 600,000 barrels per day of crude oil in 2015. But is that enough storage?

The industry does not think so. Or at least at $100 per barrel oil it did not think so. In 2015, NuStar added another 400,000 barrels of storage and Plains and Enterprise are constructing a new terminal with more than two million barrels of storage which is expected to come on line in 2018.

In nearby Ingleside, Occidental is constructing an oil terminal to handle both LPG's and crude oil exports which could add another couple of million barrels of storage. Whether Cheniere goes through with their liquids terminal is still an open question.

It seems these days that the Houston area is awash in crude oil and its coming from everywhere. Not only is there more crude oil heading to Houston, it is of varying qualities and coming from different directions. All of which means that one needs more logistics to move it around and meet the requirements of refiners, traders, pipeline company shipping schedules and vessel dock windows.

From the south, Houston can receive crude oil from the Eagle Ford, Kinder Morgan and Enterprise Pipeline systems. From the Permian Basin, Magellan and Plains own and operate major truck lines while Enterprise is building a new Permian Basin pipeline, coming on stream next year. Cushing is now connected to Houston via the Seaway Pipeline system. Houston can receive crude oil from Canada and North Dakota from Enbridge's Flanagan South Pipeline. Soon Houston will receive additional quantities of crude oil via the TransCanada Cushing Market Link by way of Beaumont/Port Arthur.

To handle all of these movements, the estimated 66 million barrels of storage at third party terminals and eight area refineries with 2.6 million barrels per day of capacity does not seem to be enough for the almost three million barrels per day of inbound pipeline refineries are still importing crude.

So, like Corpus Christi, the industry has asked for, and is getting, more storage. The most notable project is the Fairway Energy

Cavern project just south of Houston adding 10 million barrels of storage in caverns in the first phase of their project, which is expected to be on line in 2017. Phase two could add another nine million barrels of storage. Meanwhile Enterprise, TransCanada, Magellan, Genesis and others are adding an additional eight million barrels of crude oil storage. Some companies are converting fuel oil tanks to store crude oil. Additional dock capacity is on the way. Magellan has announced more capacity at Galena Park coming on line in 2018 while the Texas Deepwater Industrial Port is developing approximately 1,000 acres on the Houston Ship Channel that could have five vessels and two barge docks.

While most of the publicity about crude oil exports goes to the Corpus Christi and Houston areas, the Beaumont Port Arthur region is seeing a significant expansion in logistics and distribution facilities. The Beaumont Port Arthur area can receive crude oil from the Permian Basin via the Sunoco Permian Express System. Cushing is directly connected to Beaumont Port Arthur by the TransCanada Cushing Market Link Pipeline and also receives oil from the Seaway Pipeline system via a lateral coming over from Houston. Energy Transfer Partners along with their partner Phillips66 is developing a pipeline system from North Dakota to the Gulf Coast while at the same time constructing the Bayou Bridge pipeline from Beaumont and Port

Arthur to Lake Charles and potentially eastward to St James.

With over 30 million barrels of terminal storage capacity and more than 2.4 million barrels of inbound pipeline capacity, Beaumont Port Arthur is seeing nothing short of a significant storage building boom. Sunoco Logistics has permits to construct over five million barrels of storage, much of which is underway, while Enterprise is building six million barrels. Phillips66 announced a seven-million-barrel expansion of its Beaumont terminal.

The current infrastructure building boom got underway years ago when crude oil prices were $100 per barrel and were forecast to go even higher. US oil production rose from 5.3 million barrels per day in 2009 and peaked in April 2015 just shy of 9.7 million barrels per day. With oil prices in the $30's, production has since declined to about 9 million barrels per day. Some tankage will always be needed for logistics and distribution.

Some tankage will be used for storage. One might look at Cushing Oklahoma, with its 20+ inbound and 12+ outbound pipeline systems for guidance. In 2006, storage tank capacity was around 32 million barrels. Today it is closer to 90 million.

In July 2014 inventory levels dropped below 18 million barrels. In February 2016 inventory exceeded 66 million.

Crude oil production levels, the relative price of crude oil in North America to other markets, the market price structure and the cost of transportation will determine whether exports will continue to grow and if more infrastructure is needed.

There used to be a simple answer. If the market was back war dated, there was too much storage. If the market was in contango, there was never enough. The answer today just got a bit more complicated. [1]

Favorable market dynamics coupled with continuing crude oil price structure volatility is proving a particular bright spot for Arc Logistics Partners.

Since acquiring its first six terminals in July 2007, Arc Logistics Partners has significantly grown its market presence in North America with a series of acquisitions, the most recent of which was in July which included a newly constructed terminal in Colorado.

International and regional market dynamics are shifting the oil and gas infrastructure business and Arc Logistics

---

[1] Andy Lipow: Keeping the US crude oil exports flowing. Tank storage magazine. Volume 12, Issue 3.2016.

Partners has its sights firmly set on expanding its market presence as well as supporting the expansion plans of new and existing customers. To that end, Arc Logistics Partners' customer-centric business model has driven the company's acquisition strategy despite the current market dynamics.

In an interview with Tank Storage Magazine, John Blanchard, President of Arc Terminals, says that the business will continue to capitalize on growth opportunities and changing market dynamics.

'Increasing North American crude oil production and new logistical requirements to move this production can generally have a favorable impact on our results but the market dynamic is location and product specific.

'As we do not own any of the crude oil and petroleum products that we handle and do not engage in the marketing of crude oil and petroleum products, we have minimal direct exposure to risks associated with fluctuating commodity prices.

'We have acquired and upgraded our assets in response to increased customer demand for long term storage and throughput services. 'Our ongoing business strategy is to expand our market position and support the expansion plans of new and existing customers, while generating stable cash flows for our unitholders from quality assets supported by long-term contracts.'

All 17 terminals, which are primarily located in the East Coast and Gulf Coast with other locations including the Midwest and west coast, are strategically connected to major US pipeline infrastructure and/or additionally are linked to crucial rail and marine access points. The recent acquisition of UET Midstream's assets, which includes a newly built terminal in Colorado (the 'Pawnee Terminal') and permitted land for the development of a new terminal (the 'Buckingham Terminal'), has enhanced its market position within one of the fastest growing production areas of the US.

It provides customers direct pipeline access to Cushing, Oklahoma, via the North East Colorado Lateral of the Pony Express Pipeline. Demand for crude oil into Cushing, Oklahoma remains strong despite volatile crude oil prices and Arc expects that the newly acquired Pawnee Terminal will continue to remain a long-term consolidation and injection point for these barrels.

'The multi-modal crude oil terminal provides support for the partnership's crude oil strategy and also expands the partnership's operating footprint into the Denver Julesburg Basin,' says Blanchard.

The recently completed acquisition was purchased by Arc Logistic Partners with the intent to increase capacity and expand capabilities and access for both new and existing customers.

As with all storage terminal operators, short-term and long-term demand for, and supply of, crude oil and petroleum products plays a key role in the operation of the assets.

Other factors include the indirect impact that crude oil and petroleum product pricing has on the demand and supply of logistics assets, such as storage as well as current and future economic conditions both regionally and globally.

'Our ability, and the ability of our competitors to capitalize on growth opportunities and changing market dynamics is another factor that impacts the local market,' adds Blanchard.

'Law and regulations affecting our business frequently change and evolve, creating a variety of challenges for any terminal operator. 'We strive to be proactive in our response to the changing regulatory environment to capitalize on these opportunities. [1]

---

[1] Keeping up with demand. Tank storage magazine. Volume 11, Issue 6.2015.

For the past few years, China has witnessed a strong growth in its demand on crude oil. In 2012, crude oil consumption reached 480 million ton, which more doubled that in 2000. With an average annual growth rate in the late 10 years of 7 %, now China has become the second largest oil consumer in the world. Due to small quantity of crude oil resource, growth rate of crude oil production is not large with only 2%in the same period. In 2012, production of crude oil in China is 207 million-ton, topping world No. 5. Since China became oil importing country in 1993, China enjoys a continuous rise in net oil import volume and a constant increase in its dependence on foreign countries. In 2012, degree of its oil dependence on foreign countries reached 56 %. [1]

---

[1] Jinjun Xue • Zhongxiu Zhao • Yande Dai • Bo Wang: Green Low-Carbon Development in China. Springer International Publishing Switzerland 2013. P 85

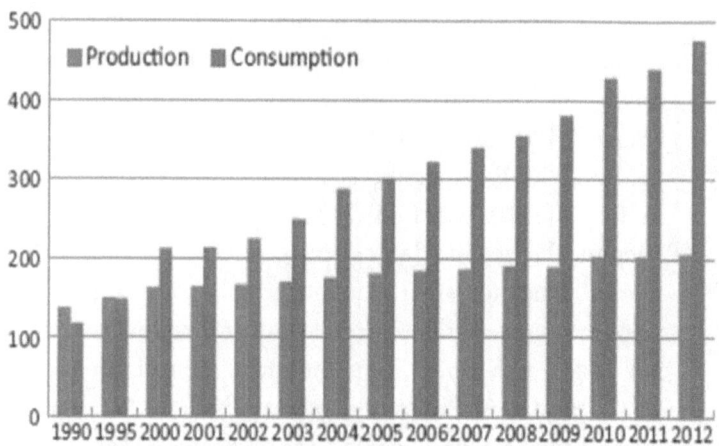

There are two mains reasons for the reduction in oil demand. The first reason is that the demand for energy is closely related to economic activity, so weaker economic activity resulted in a fall in demand for oil. The second channel that led to shrunken oil demand is not related to economic activity but comes from monetary policy. [1]

2.2. oil supply

The price of oil is important because as this rises exploration is encouraged and oil that was previously uneconomic can be brought to market. Economists have made much of this dynamic, though usually citing the flawed apparent replacement of the proved reserves data to prove their case. The proper question is: At a

---

[1] Naoyuki Yoshino • Farhad Taghizadeh-Hesary: Monetary Policy and the Oil Market. Asian Development Bank Institute 2016. P 3

given oil price by how much can conventional oil production increase?

The detailed answer must come from reservoir engineers; and is also a function of date as technology advances with time. Some answers by field have been illustrated above, and we have also partial answers at least by region (and also globally) from the roughly decade of high oil prices (above $50/bbl in today's money) from 1974 to 1985, and a second decade of prices above this level from 2005 to 2015. Based on these data—for example, for US Lower-48 production over the first period, and the UK production for the current period—the answer is 'by not much', though admittedly the economists may have a valid point in saying that a decade is probably not enough for new exploration plays and production paradigms to come fully into effect.

Overall however, on the above field data and regional data, it would seem unwise to expect a high price, even $100/bbl, to bring on very much in the way of extra conventional oil. Moreover, the price cannot go too high: as we know fairly solidly from both the earlier and the current period of high oil prices, that a price much above $50/bbl in today's money slows economic activity and reduces oil demand at least in the developed countries; while above about $100/bbl in real terms it would seem to lead to global recession. [1]

The world's petroleum liquids supply — boosted by a tight oil, condensate and NGL output surge from US unconventional sources — was higher in 2014, with total growth of 2.20 mb/d compared with 0.58 mb/d in 2013. Non-OPEC oil producers from all OECD regions saw good growth in 2014 for the first time in recent years, which led to a rise of 1.87 mb/d to average 24.12 mb/d. Moreover, the oil supply from developing countries, the former Soviet Union and China increased by 0.21 mb/d, 0.02 mb/d and 0.03 mb/d, respectively. The non-OPEC liquids supply increased by 2.17 mb/d, followed by OPEC NGLs at 0.18 mb/d to total an average of 62.32 mb/d. OPEC crude production averaged 30.07 mb/d in 2014. The total world oil supply averaged 92.4 mb/d, with OPEC's crude share standing at 32.6 per cent compared with 33.5 per cent one year earlier.

Non-OPEC supply averaged 56.49 mb/d in 2014, an increase of 2.17 mb/d over the previous year. Growth was driven by a rise from OECD Americas — with the US being the main contributor, followed by Canada — and other regions, including Brazil, Russia, Norway, the Sudan, Australia, Malaysia and China. Declines from Mexico, Indonesia, Syria, Kazakhstan and Azerbaijan partially offset growth. [1]

([1])R.W. Bentley: Introduction to Peak Oil. Springer International Publishing Switzerland 2016. P 52: 53

([1])Organization of the Petroleum Exporting Countries.

On a regional basis, OECD's oil supply increased by 1.87 mb/d in 2014 over the previous year to average 24.12 mb/d. Much of the OECD's growth in supply came from OECD Americas, which experienced the greatest growth among all non-OPEC regions in 2014 at 1.82 mb/d. OECD Asia Pacific and OECD Europe experienced relatively good growth in 2014 at 0.03 mb/d and 0.02 mb/d, respectively. The US experienced the highest growth in oil supply among all non- OPEC countries in 2014, up by 1.64 mb/d, supported by a surge in tight oil production from shale development areas. Additionally, Canada's oil supply saw strong growth of 0.27 mb/d in 2014, while Mexico encountered a minor decline of 0.09 mb/d compared with the previous year. Oil production in the North Sea increased mainly in Norway and the UK, where it was boosted by 140 tb/d and 70 tb/d, respectively, compared with one year earlier. Australia's oil supply also experienced an increase of 30 tb/d in 2014; indeed, it was up by 100 tb/d over the previous year's decline of 70 tb/d.

Oil production in developing countries (DCs) grew by 0.21 mb/d in 2014, mainly in Latin America, to average 12.69 mb/d compared with one year earlier. The Other Asia and Middle East regions experienced supply declines in 2014, while Africa and Latin America

---

Annual Report 2014. P 17: 19

registered production growth. Relative growth by Colombia and Brazil in Latin America compared with initial forecasts impacted total DC growth in 2014. The Sudan's oil supply was up by 0.05 mb/d, showing the largest increase among all African countries, reaching 0.29 mb/d. OECD growth was approximately equal to the declines experienced in other countries such as Syria and Yemen in the Middle East, Indonesia, Brunei, India and Malaysia in Other Asia, Argentina in Latin America and minor declines in Congo, Gabon and South Africa on the African continent.

The Former Soviet Union (FSU)'s oil supply experienced growth of only 0.02 mb/d in 2014, to average 13.43 mb/d. Most of Russia's growth was offset by annual declines in Kazakhstan and Azerbaijan. Chinese oil production increased by 30 tb/d in 2014 to average 4.32 mb/d. [1]

---

[1] Organization of the Petroleum Exporting Countries. Annual Report 2014. P 19

OPEC crude oil production based on secondary sources, 2010-14 *(1,000 b/d)*

	2010	2011	2012	2013	1Q14	2Q14	3Q14	4Q14	2014	Average change 2014/13
Algeria	1,250	1,240	1,210	1,159	1,128	1,158	1,167	1,152	1,151	-7
Angola	1,786	1,667	1,738	1,738	1,600	1,646	1,705	1,688	1,660	-78
Ecuador	475	490	499	516	537	541	543	546	542	26
IR Iran	3,706	3,628	2,977	2,673	2,774	2,768	2,759	2,763	2,766	93
Iraq	2,401	2,665	2,979	3,037	3,217	3,266	3,153	3,424	3,265	228
Kuwait	2,297	2,538	2,793	2,822	2,797	2,786	2,794	2,719	2,774	-48
Libya	1,559	462	1,393	928	371	222	614	679	473	-455
Nigeria	2,061	2,111	2,073	1,912	1,901	1,892	1,949	1,904	1,911	0
Qatar	791	794	753	732	733	725	724	682	716	-15
Saudi Arabia	8,254	9,296	9,737	9,586	9,702	9,675	9,747	9,608	9,683	97
UAE	2,304	2,516	2,624	2,741	2,745	2,749	2,791	2,757	2,761	19
Venezuela	2,370	2,413	2,392	2,389	2,381	2,377	2,369	2,364	2,373	-16
Total OPEC	29,255	29,821	31,168	30,231	29,885	29,805	30,316	30,286	30,075	-157

(1)

The price of oil is partly determined by actual supply and demand, and partly by expectations. Part of the recent price collapse

---

(¹)data services dep. 2016

can be attributed to a new glut in oil supply. Unconventional energy resources, such as shale oil, shale gas, and oil sands, have raised the global oil supply. Massive discoveries of oil in North Dakota and Texas in the US have driven down prices, even amid tensions in the Middle East and Ukraine, and roughly three million more barrels a day are being produced now than in 2011.

In addition to this, while oil prices were falling, the Organization of the Petroleum Exporting Countries (OPEC), which controls nearly 40 % of the world market, failed to reach an agreement on production curbs at a meeting in Vienna on 27 November 2104, sending the price down even further. [1]

2.3. Natural gas demand

The different nature of gas makes its pricing system differ from that of oil. Natural gas is not only priced differently but the nature of the commodity almost separated natural gas that was delivered via pipelines from liquid natural gas (LNG) into separate commodities, although both are ultimately gas.

As natural gas is exactly that—gas—it cannot simply be put in a barrel and brought to a spot auction. It can only be transported in tightly

---

[1] Naoyuki Yoshino • Farhad Taghizadeh-Hesary: Monetary Policy and the Oil Market. Asian Development Bank Institute 2016. P 2: 3

sealed pipelines that were built to a specific destination. Because of the costs involved in bringing gas from its source to its markets by building pipelines and the accompanying infrastructure, that investment had to be guaranteed when pipeline projects were contemplated so that natural gas tends to be delivered under long-term contracts to ensure that the projects are commercially viable.

As gas is associated with oil, the price of gas shadows the price of oil in most contracts. There are some exceptions such as Yemen's LNG contracts with the companies GDF Suez (now Engie) and Total. Those exports were initially meant to go to the USA and so were indexed to American prices based on Henry Hub gas trading. The US pricing system for natural gas is unique as it is based on futures trading. The other main regional markets are Europe and Asia. Indexing natural gas to the price of oil originated in Europe in the 1960s and was the system adopted by Asia to price its natural gas imports. Since the two systems are completely different ways of pricing the commodity, the prices for American gas and European or Asian gas are often different. Owing to the increased supply of US natural gas from fracking, by 2014 it cost about a quarter of what Russian gas cost and was spurring Europeans to push for a new pricing formula for their gas which would take spot market prices into account more.

Since the USA is no longer importing as much LNG as was expected in the early years of the twenty-first century, much of the gas Yemen had earmarked for the USA gets exported to Asia with Yemen sharing in the profits. The pricing structure tying the price of gas to oil limits the gas markets to regions accessible by pipelines or LNG ports and their associated pipelines. Th e European region is largely supplied by Russia in Central Europe and Algeria in the Iberian Peninsula, while the North American region saw exchanges of gas between the USA, Canada, and Mexico. Starting in the 1960s, LNG exports expanded that trade with Algeria supplying Europe and the USA supplying Japan with Alaskan gas.

Although those natural gas exports were being shipped under contracts, there were still occasions when there were energy surpluses, which would be sold on spot markets, and also shortfalls when distributors who had more demand than they contracted for wanted to buy additional gas. Western Europe has a number of gas trading hubs, the largest of which is the UK National Balancing Point, developed in the mid-1990s when spot prices for natural gas were as much as 30% below long-term contract prices, giving the same impetus to setting up a natural gas futures exchange as the early 1980s had experienced in the oil markets. In 2010, some 25% of natural gas sales in Europe were done through spot markets along those hubs, yet that volume was not sufficient to turn the hubs into price-setting mechanisms, and most gas was still delivered based on contracts that linked the price of gas to oil, even though the Europeans were expressing a preference for seeing the market set prices over long-term contracts.

Asia consumes about 60% of the world's LNG trade, and Japan, Korea, and Taiwan all based their prices on the Japan Crude Cocktail oil-indexed price mechanism, which took the top crudes imported by Japan as the benchmark for pricing gas and LNG. In China, the government announced plans in 2011 to reform the price of natural gas to consumers by pegging the price of natural gas to alternative forms of energy. As gas was subsidized, despite the decline of the price of oil, consumers have not seen natural gas prices decrease. India has multiple regional pricing regimes. Th e price of domestically produced natural gas brought online by state companies is set by the government, while imported gas is determined by the market.

Although Europe and Asia continued to use long-term contracts tied to the price of oil as the primary price-setting mechanism, things worked differently in the USA. In 1989, natural gas futures began being traded on the floor at NYMEX and in April 1990 they became a formally traded commodity on the exchange. Th e contracts were pegged to the spot price for gas at the Henry Hub distribution center in Louisiana, where 13 pipelines intersected to supply the USA with some 5 billion cubic feet (1.8 billion cubic meters) of gas each day. Th e futures trading differentiated how gas was priced in the US when compared to Europe or Asia. With the advent of fracking towards the end of the first decade of the twenty-first century and the release of enormous deposits of gas from shale, the US market found it was well supplied with gas, and that was reflected in the price, which dropped to half of what it had been in 2008 (NYMEX). Countries in the EU have been seeking a formula, which would take the futures price of gas, as well as the spot market price, into account in pricing the commodity. But as of 2015, the contract price for gas sold to the EU was still tied to long-term deals that include infrastructure costs. [1]

With the technological improvement in natural gas storage, the trade in natural gas has increased sharply. Now there are three major natural gas trading markets, which are based on the European pipeline transportation systems, Asia-Pacific LNG transportation network, and the North American pipeline transportation systems. The US, Germany, and Italy are the top

[1] Thijs Van de Graaf • Benjamin K. Sovacool Arunabha Ghosh • Florian Kern • Michael T. Klare: The Palgrave Handbook of the International Political Economy of Energy. 2016. P 236: 238

three natural gas importers in the world, with combined imports representing 38 % of the world total (2008). Japan is the largest LNG import country at 95.4 billion cubic meters in 2008, or 42 % of the world total. As a better and more environment-friendly energy source than coal and petroleum, natural gas is expected to keep developing quickly in the next three decades. China, India, and other Asia-Pacific countries have shown considerable market potential and their shares of natural gas have much room for growth. [1]

Chinese natural gas demand has turned from high-speed development to middle-speed development in a short period of time, creating significant uncertainties in global gas markets.

On the one hand, since electricity demand is slowing down as a result of slowing economic growth, the volume of natural gas consumed in China by gas-fired power stations, especially peaking power stations, was lower

than estimated in 2014. On the other hand, gas price is the key element influencing the development of gas-fired power stations. In China, the price of electricity is regulated by the central government, which has not fully considered the environmentally friendly and

---

[1] Yi-Ming Wei • Hua Liao: Energy Economics: Energy Efficiency in China. Springer International Publishing Switzerland 2016. P 23

load-following advantages of gas-fired power stations. Considering that the average generation cost of a gas-fired power station is twice that of a coal-fired power station, it is difficult for gas-fired power plants to generate at full capacity. Thus, even if a great increment of gas-fired station capacity is installed, the volume of natural gas consumed may be small due to low plant use factors.

For the industrial sector, taking into account the relatively lower price of coal, implementing the 'coal-to-gas' project is difficult for companies unless the government strongly encourages an increase in the utilization of cleaner energy and is willing to pay substantial subsidies. [1]

---

[1] Leo Lester: Energy Relations and Policy Making in Asia. 2016. P 137: 138

The global natural gas market

The global natural gas market includes the pipeline gas market and the liquefied natural gas market

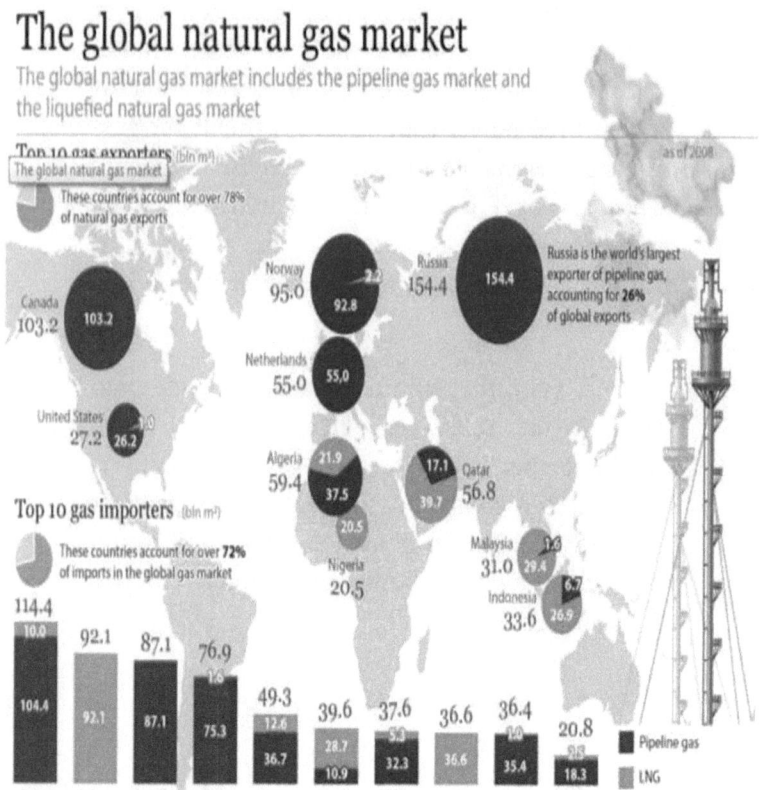

Note that the list of the top producers is different from the list of top exporters, because some countries produce a lot and consume a lot i.e. USA, and some others produce a lot but do not consume that much i.e. Russia.

Obviously, this is something that has to do with the size of the economy. At the following map from the Financial Times you can see the largest importers of natural gas in 2011, after the nuclear accident of Fukushima (Japan). Now Japan is the top importer of expensive LNG. The table also shows the top exporters. You can see that the United States is included in the list of exporters, because the US exports gas to Mexico and Canada, when this is more convenient geographically, but the US imports far more from these two countries in oil and gas. (1)

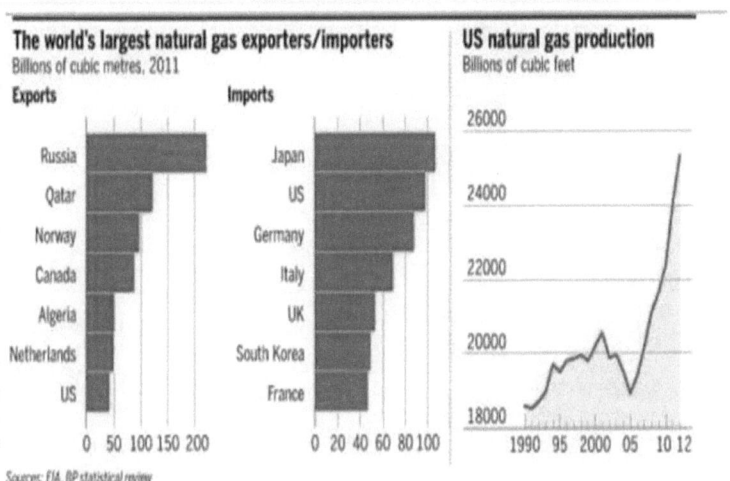

At the following map from Indexmundi you can see the top importers of gas in 2013 (1st January 2014). You can see Russia and the Netherlands in the list, because even though they are among the top exporters they

---

(¹)Iakovos Alhadeff: Energy & Terrorism Part 3. Free ebook.net 2016. P 6

also import gas i.e. Russia from Turkmenistan and the Netherlands from UK and Norway. [1]

Rank Country	Natural gas - imports (cubic meters)
1 Japan	122,199,998,464
2 United States	88,770,002,944
3 Germany	87,960,002,560
4 Italy	67,799,998,464
5 China	52,999,999,488
6 Slovakia	50,180,001,792
7 United Kingdom	48,260,001,792
8 France	47,709,999,104
9 Korea, South	47,339,999,232
10 Turkey	45,920,002,048
11 Ukraine	44,800,000,000
12 Austria	42,560,000,000
13 Belgium	38,899,998,720
14 Poland	37,380,001,792
15 Spain	36,750,000,128
16 Russia	32,500,000,768
17 Canada	31,310,000,128
18 Netherlands	24,650,000,384
19 Belarus	21,020,000,256
20 United Arab Emirates	17,440,000,000

Definition: This entry is the total natural gas imported in cubic meters (cu m).

Source: CIA World Factbook - Unless otherwise noted, information in this page is accurate as of January 1, 2014

In China, demand for natural gas is very strong, especially with increasing control of air pollution, with many regions showing extraordinary growth. Annual gas consumption is growing faster than production, so gas supply is very tight, and ensuring supply for the peak

---

[1] Iakovos Alhadeff: Energy & Terrorism Part 3. Free ebook.net 2016. P 7

gas consumption in the winter heating period seems to be difficult.

To ensure the safe use of gas, gas turbine supply is restricted. For the sake of protecting the gas supply, China raised the price of natural gas for non-residents, but the country has not formed a unified mechanism of gas turbine power generation price, and some enterprises continue to experience losses due to generation cost increase and inadequate local subsidies. [1]

After several years of stagnation, gas demand has increased (+2%), thanks to the rising penetration of gas in China and India, but also thanks to the strong growth in Europe (Germany, France, UK, etc.), allowed by a renewed competitiveness in relation to coal. Gas has also continued to replace coal in the USA (+1%) and has stabilized in Russia. Eventually, 2016 saw a significant increase in LNG market volumes, thanks in particular to the capacity increases in Australia. [2]

The supply of natural gas worldwide has increased by 25 per cent between 2000 and

---

[1] Zhongfu TAN, Kangting CHEN, Liwei JU, Pingkuo LIU, Chen ZHANG: Issues and solutions of China's generation resource utilization based on sustainable development. J. Mod. Power Syst. Clean Energy. 2016. P 149: 150

[2] Enerdata : The energy mix remains overly carbon intensive despite the slight decrease of coal. 2017. P 2

2008 (from 80 trillion cubic feet per annum (Tcfpa) to 102 Tcfpa) and is expected to increase to over 140 Tcfpa by 2020, as illustrated in Figure 6.1. In

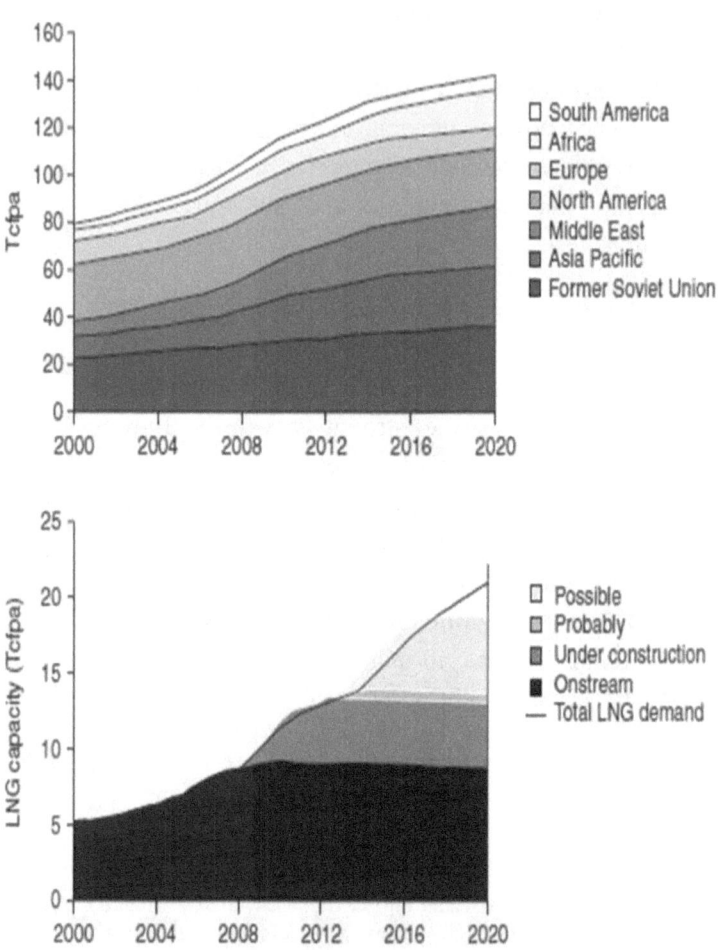

the same period the amount of gas volumes traded as LNG has doubled (from 5

Tcfpa to 10 Tcfpa and is expected to double again by 2020 (~20 Tcfpa) as shown in Figure 6.2, taking LNG's contribution to overall supply from 6 per cent in 2000 to 14 per cent in 2020.

The Figure illustrates the extent of the divergence between the regions which own the remaining gas resources and those which currently consume the most gas. Seventy per cent of remaining proven reserves is in the former Soviet Union and Middle East, which currently account for only 30 per cent of consumption.

By contrast, Europe and North America make up nearly half of global current consumption but have only 8 per cent of remaining reserves. This picture may change if the perceived scale – and commerciality – of the recent shale gas discoveries in the US becomes proven.

The opportunity for new LNG projects to meet the growing dependence on imported gas in the main demand centers has stimulated the industry's appetite

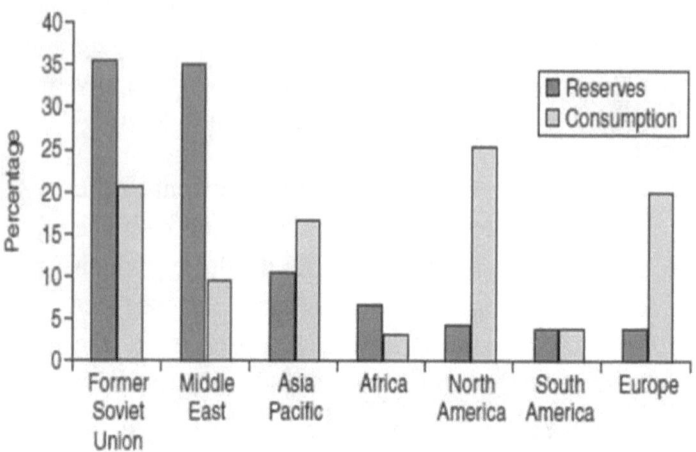

for gas in resource-rich countries and companies are increasingly keen to acquire gas reserves. A major stumbling block for them is the fact that gas reserves remain largely under state control in many of these countries. The inability of domestic consumers to pay anything like the gas prices received in the developed countries has traditionally meant that local gas projects have largely been developed by governments, which have taken ownership of the gas reserves. The emergence of export markets for gas mean that governments are now keen for increased export revenues but remain equally keen that abundant local gas supplies replace oil and other primary fuels in power generation and industrial projects and contribute to the expansion of these activities. To promote investment in domestic projects, therefore, some governments have begun to tie investor's rights to export gas with obligations to develop local gas projects.

The ability of governments and industry to meet growing domestic and export demand for natural gas is influenced by many factors such as exploration success, LNG marketing advantages, corporate positions and geopolitics – all of which are uncertain and subject to change. Where the parties can influence outcomes is in the design of an appropriate taxation policy to ensure risks are balanced by rewards along the value chain. The design of a suitable fiscal policy for natural gas presents government with a number of simultaneous policy issues. [1]

2.4. Natural Gas supply

North American natural gas supplies have seen a remarkable increase since 2006, with the rapid expansion of horizontal drilling and hydraulic fracturing. Although the estimates of economically available gas supplies vary widely, there is general agreement that the recent U.S. shale gas boom will continue into the foreseeable future. Naturally, the increased supplies have led to a reduction in price, and even the long-range projections of the gas price have come down from previous projections of just a few years ago. [2]

([1])Philip Daniel, Michael Keen and Charles McPherson: The Taxation of Petroleum and Minerals. international Monetary Fund. 2010. P 163: 165

Natural gas use has recently seen dramatic increases in the electric power sector, with a corresponding reduction in the share of electricity generated from coal.

Beyond the power generation demands for natural gas, there is an extensive search for new markets where natural gas may compete effectively with other energy sources. For example, there is potential for increased direct use of natural gas in transportation. Natural gas use in the transportation sector is currently relatively small but may increase dramatically if the necessary infrastructure is put in place.

There is a possibility for indirect use of natural gas, via transformation of natural gas to a liquid fossil fuel, such as diesel. The industrial sector, already a large user of gas, will probably experience an increase in exports and production, due to increasing competitiveness from cheaper natural gas. Sectors that use gas heavily as an energy input or a feedstock, such as fertilizers and inorganic chemicals, are already showing new signs of life. This has led to the characterization of the current stimulus in manufacturing as a "U.S. Manufacturing Renaissance". Finally, US natural gas may eventually be exported on a large scale, if liquefied natural gas (LNG) facilities are built

---

[2]Rossella Bardazzi • Maria Grazia Pazienza Alberto Tonini: European Energy and Climate Security. Springer International Publishing Switzerland 2016. P 113

quickly enough. Price-driven substitution of gas for other fuels is expected to be occurring worldwide, leading to an increase in demand by gas importing countries. In the short-run, the export potential is constrained by the capacity of existing LNG transport facilities, but with sufficient investment, this constraint will be ameliorated over time. Finally, substitution may occur in the residential market, with substitution of natural gas for electricity. [1]

natural gas supply is a predominantly regional energy source. Even with the recent increases in Liquefied Natural Gas facilities and tankers about 90 % of NG supply is still delivered through pipelines. The exploitation of natural gas fields had to wait for the pipeline infrastructure to be put in place in the post-WWII period, thus, a peak in overall natural gas production is at least a decade away. [2]

Although conventional natural gas production has peaked in North America, shale gas production has more than offset conventional well depletion in the past few years. As with shale oil though, the long-term viability of shale gas production has been questioned given low per well production, high depletion rates, and the relatively small "sweet

---

[1]Rossella Bardazzi • Maria Grazia Pazienza Alberto Tonini: European Energy and Climate Security. Springer International Publishing Switzerland 2016. P 114
[2]Roger Boyd: Energy and the Financial System Springer Cham Heidelberg New York Dordrecht London 2013. P 34

spots" within shale gas areas. Some of the earlier shale gas plays do seem to have peaked, or be nearing peak, supporting those that see shale gas as a short-term palliative rather than a long-term replacement for North American gas supplies. If this view is true, the USA may again become a net gas importer before 2020. The US production levels over the next few years will demonstrate whether such an outcome is likely. The increased production volumes may also be somewhat misleading given that the net energy provided by shale gas is significantly lower than that for conventional gas. Thus, the gas production numbers may overstate the increase in available net energy. [1]

The lack of the infrastructure to export gas from North America, together with US government restrictions on gas exports, has meant that the increased shale gas production has led to a regional glut and low prices. In many cases, shale gas production is not profitable at current regional prices. The lower prices have led to a displacement of coal for electricity generation, as many plants can burn either coal or natural gas, and new natural gas capable plants are being added. Shale gas production has also displaced the expected the US LNG imports, and thus, reduced the global competition for such supplies.

---

[1] Roger Boyd: Energy and the Financial System Springer Cham Heidelberg New York Dordrecht London 2013. P 34

European conventional natural gas production has, or will have very shortly, peaked. Large-scale imports from Russia, together with supplies from North Africa, have become a significant part of the European energy supplies. LNG supplies from the Middle East are also increasing. Shale gas production is now being explored as a way to reduce dependence on these external supplies but is at a much earlier stage of development than North America and costs will also be higher due to more dense populations, more difficult geology, and stronger environmental legislation. In addition, the extensive energy extraction infrastructure that could be easily utilized within the USA is not present in the European countries. Thus, shale gas may have much less of an impact than in North America. [1]

From 1973, during the oil embargo, to 1984, the price of natural gas (NG) rose 12-fold, while US output declined by 15 %. From 2001 through 2007 the price of NG rose 50 %. This provided the financial incentive for innovation. The entrepreneurial pioneer of fracking in Texas was Mitchell Energy and Development Company, which applied the technology on the Barnett Shale. During those years fracking was very profitable.

([1])Roger Boyd: Energy and the Financial System Springer Cham Heidelberg New York Dordrecht London 2013. P 34

Then, rather suddenly, NG prices dropped dramatically in 2008 (due to oversupply) and have since remained below the cost of drilling and operating new wells. Since then, demand from the electric power industry, has helped NG prices recover somewhat, but in summer 2014 they were still below breakeven, despite near-zero interest rates. But the low prices have given an economic boost to the US economy, badly needed in the post-2008 era.

There has been a lot of hype. One fracking optimist is Ed Morse, head of commodity research for Citigroup, frequently interviewed on CNBC and quoted in the Wall Street Journal (WSJ). Others include Porter Stansbury ("The Oil Report"), and the notorious "activist investor"—some would say "corporate raider"—H. Boone Pickens, who also gets interviewed on TV a lot. Pickens is a cheerleader for "Saudi America". Morse thinks US oil production will surpass that of Saudi Arabia by 2020, based on continued growth of the shale "fracking" sector (and oil from Canadian tar sands). He foresaw declining US demand (due to increasing efficiency) and a declining rate of economic growth rate in China, resulting in an "oil glut" by 2020 with prices down by 20% from 2011 levels.

(His forecast was too conservative.) The US Energy Information Agency (USEIA) and the International Energy Agency (IEA) both accepted this view. Nothing has happened to change the "official" view since then.

The profitability of fracking for gas is now in question, partly because several of the early leaders were losing money even when oil prices were higher. Four of the main shale gas and oil producers (Chesapeake, Devon, Southwestern and EOG) lost a cumulative total of $42 million during the 5-year period from 2008-through 2012.

(Chesapeake cancelled its dividend in July 2015). Of course, they still have assets, but many firms have had to write-down their claimed gas reserves. Contrarian energy analyst Bill Powers has noted that some of the shale startups booked reserves based on claimed well lifetimes of up to 40–65 years (Powers 2013). Yet most shale wells exhibit rapid decline in production. Typical Bakken shale oil wells, starting at 500 bbl/day, were down to 150 bbl/day at the end of 12 months, 90 bbl/day after 24 months 50 bbl/day after 48 months and continuing to nearly zero after 5 years (Hughes 2010).

The natural gas price collapse in late 2008 was partly due to the global collapse of oil prices in that year and partly to the recession that followed the financial storm.

This prompted a massive shift from shale gas to shale oil, partly based on the sharp recovery in the price of crude oil after the deep dip in 2008-9. But the problem of rapid depletion of shale wells remains. There are "sweet spots" but no gushers to counterbalance the large number of dry wells. Very few wells in a typical field are highly productive. For instance, about 30% of wells yield less than 250 bbl/day at a given time, while 30% produced more than 500 bbl/day and perhaps 3% produced more than 1000 bbl/day. This depletion rate means that just to maintain current output requires far more drilling than conventional oil or gas fields. [1]

The World Energy Council's Resources 2013 chapter on natural gas predicted natural gas could reach 25% of the global energy mix by 2030. Unconventional gas supplies have the potential to reflect a substantial portion of that share and will continue to change the supply landscape for natural gas. The US shale gas revolution serves as a unique case study that demonstrates how suppliers can use technology innovation to drive to more affordable and secure supplies of natural gas. However, the reality remains that current market dynamics place the future of natural gas at risk. Swift intervention is needed by key market actors to protect long-term conventional and unconventional supplies. [2]

[1]Robert Ayres: ENERGY, COMPLEXITY AND WEALTH MAXIMIZATION. Springer International Publishing Switzerland 2016. P 318: 320

The benchmark spot price, the British market NBP, reached €20/MWh in 2015, down by 5% from 2014 - a background trend which started at the beginning of 2013 (€27/MWh), before the drop in the oil price from mid-2014. In dollar terms, this price stands at $6.5/MBtu, a 21% fall, due to the weakness of the euro (-16% in 2015).

2015 was notable in the United Kingdom for the renewed competitiveness of gas compared to coal - the price of which is falling significantly by 25% in $/t and 9% in €/t. This change is partly due to the

increase in the "Carbon Tax Support", which has been fixed since April 2015 at £18/tCO2 (€25/tCO2) as against £9.5/tCO2 in 2014. This mechanism has also had the effect of supporting the price of electricity, which ensures the profitability of gas power plants. This is not the case in the rest of Europe, where the price of CO2, regulated only by the quotas market, is still low, at a 2015 average of €8/tCO2.

At the beginning of January, futures markets are capitalizing on a NBP price which is once again falling in 2016, estimated at about €15/MWh, or $4.7/MBtu - close to the prevailing conditions in 2009/2010. It is possible that it will rise towards the market equivalent

---

[2] World Energy Resources. World Energy Council. 2016. P 5

price with coal of €18/MWh ($5.7/MBtu) and may exceed that price should there be tensions in the market (harsh winter, etc.).

Regarding the continent's long-term contracts, each year they are coming closer to conditions prevailing on the spot markets. So, in France, the CRE (Commission de Régulation de l'Energie) considered since July 2015 a 77% share for spot prices to determine the supply costs. They are therefore, increasingly correlated with spot prices. [1]

In most countries and especially the rapid growing economies of the Far East and some Gulf States, governments and utility companies invest in energy infrastructure to facilitate economic growth. With the growth of industry, there is an increasing need for commercial energy based on oil, natural gas or coal. So, it is needed to have an energy supply system that is technically good and economically efficient including price. Natural gas price is not easy to determine because it is not a perfect substitute for other fuels for its high transmission costs and its depletion. [2]

In the future, China's natural gas is expected to enjoy a fast development. It is

---

[1] Investments in exploration/production and refining 2015. IFP Energies Nouvelles - January 2016. P 8
[2] PROF. DR. ENG H. FARAG/ ENG. A, ELMISSIRIEGUIDELINES FOR EVALUATION OF NATURAL GAS PROJECTS. P 1

estimated that, by 2020, natural gas utilization volume will reach 300 billion cubic meters. Natural gas development strategy of China in next 10 years is: strengthen domestic natural gas exploration, boost the rapid growth of conventional production of natural gas, promote the development and utilization of unconventional natural gas resources including coal bed gas, shale gas etc, search for overseas natural gas supply to realize a safe and stable supply of natural gas. [1]

2.5. Oil and Gas Production Costs

Detailed oil and gas production costs are difficult to find. Data collected from conventional oil and gas fields in Europe show a wide spread of operating and capital costs. In 2009, production costs for conventional oil ranged from 3.00 to 35.00 USD per barrel of oil equivalent (BOE), with the majority being around 15 USD/BOE. The conventional gas production costs ranged from 0.50 to 3.75 USD per thousand cubic feet (MCF), with the majority costing around 0.90 USD/MCF. The cost figures include capital and operating costs, including a rate of return on invested capital, but do not include taxes and royalties.

Some of the cost estimates refer to relatively shallow and favorable production

[1] Jinjun Xue • Zhongxiu Zhao • Yande Dai • Bo Wang: Green Low-Carbon Development in China. Springer International Publishing Switzerland 2013. P 99

conditions, while deep offshore production, for instance, can be significantly higher. Cost of oil and gas production is influenced by factors such as geological conditions, depth of accumulations, regulatory environments, and project lengths. Offshore capital cost increases at greater depths are mainly due to the higher cost of platform drilling, the cost of new technology to cope with depressurization of reservoirs, and the cost of pipeline transportation. Nevertheless, considerable cost savings have been achieved over the past decades on account of improved operating methods.

Longer term projections of oil and gas production costs should account for the cost-reducing effects of improved technology versus the cost-increasing effects of depletion. As oil and gas fields at shallow depths will likely be exploited first (assuming suitable market and regulatory conditions), there will be a gradual shift towards deeper drilling, including offshore, as well as a shift towards unconventional sources of oil and gas. This will require increased investment costs for new wells and higher operating expenditures due to additional costs for enhanced recovery. In the absence of advanced innovation, these factors are likely to drive up long-run production costs. However, though the past is not always an indication of the future, history would suggest that producers may develop the technologies needed to offset the cost-increasing effects of deeper, more remote, and increasingly unconventional resources. For example, the costs of producing unconventional oil and gas have been lowered to the point of being comparable in some cases to the development of the conventional. In this study, a uniform production cost is applied to each of the unconventional sources. [1]

Cost is a major determinant factor as well as an indicator of price; it represents a resistance point to the lowering of price. The effectiveness of an organization is reflected to some extent on its ability to hold down the overall controllable cost. It is desirable to minimize the cost of an organization through better utilization of resources and prudent economic and operational decisions. E&P business is associated with high-cost activities and holding down the base cost is one of the main concerns of E&P companies across the world. *The total cost is the sum of statutory cost (government taxes, duties, and levies) and operating cost that includes the cost for amortization, depletion, depreciation, impairment loss, and operational cost, besides general administrative expenses*:

Total cost = statutory cost + operating cost

$\begin{pmatrix} \text{including amortization, depletion, depreciation, impairment loss,} \\ \text{G \& A, and other operational costs} \end{pmatrix}$

---

[1] Walter Leal Filho • Vlasios Voudouris: Global Energy Policy and Security. Springer-Verlag London 2013. P 147

Statutory cost consists of various taxes, duties, and levies imposed by the government such as royalty, levies, and local and central taxes. In addition, corporate tax is charged by the government on the profit of the company. An E&P company has little control on the statutory cost imposed by the government, which is a major source of government revenue. The amount of statutory cost varies from country to country and is quite high in oil-exporting countries. It is the main source of income of these countries and accounts for more than 80% of the gross revenue (or over 95% of the total cost).

The analysis of 10 years of cost data of an E&P company in an oil-importing country reveals that the statutory cost accounts for approximately 20% of gross revenue (or ~30% of the total cost). This may be indicative of many other oil-importing nations.

Operating cost *is the sum of amortization, depletion, impairment loss, depreciation, and other operational costs.* Amortization means recovery of expenses in part through the year's revenue for those fields, which have either been abandoned or are at the exploratory stage or whose commercial viability is yet to be determined.

Depletion can be defined as the prorated value assigned to the extinction of natural resources, that is, oil and gas. It is difficult to prorate expenditure incurred on exploration, development of field, reserves accretion, and so on, on unit basis for the purpose of long term plan. It is depleted according to policies followed by the respective E&P companies, which may change from time to time. In addition, there is impairment loss that occurs when the cost of holding the asset exceeds its fair market value. In other words, it is the amount by which the carrying amount of an asset exceeds its recoverable amount.

Depreciation is a source of fund and is created by charging wear and tear and obsolescence cost at a predetermined rate.

Other operational costs include the expenditure incurred toward the operation of workover rig, water injection, research and development, foreign contracts, transportation of oil and gas, and so on. [1]

Therefore,

---

[1] Sanjib Chowdhury: Optimization and Business Improvement Studies in Upstream Oil and Gas Industry. John Wiley & Sons, Inc. 2016. P 295

$$Qx_2 \le b_2; \quad \text{or,} \quad x_2 \le \frac{b_2}{Q}$$

where

b_2 = total cost

x_2 = unit cost of production of oil and oil equivalent gas

The oil markets are integrated to such a point that major events impacting oil producing countries affect the crude oil prices worldwide. oil prices have been relatively stable in real terms between 1986 and 2003 as growth in consumption was matched by growth in production and technological improvement. Shocks on prices disappeared with either the cause of the shock or because other oil producers managed to increase their production. Between 2003 and 2013, oil prices have fluctuated more violently. First, the addition of the Iraq war with growth in crude oil demand from rapidly developing countries and the failure to increase production at the same rate as the demand, generated an energy crisis where the theme of peak oil became popular. The 2008 financial crisis resulted in a violent market correction which was short lived as global economy started its recovery. The Arab Spring pressured oil prices upward since crude oil production was largely disrupted in that country and because of the importance of Libya in the oil production market. The strength of the shock is, once again, due mostly to the very low-price elasticity of the oil commodity and to the quasi-absence of substitutes.

Formally, natural gas prices are subjects to four main characteristics. first, supply and demand levels naturally play an important role in refining natural gas prices. The role played by major events on demand and supply should be clear after what has been written previously on coal and oil. For example, at least part of the drop-in prices in the second part of 2008 can be attributed to decreasing industrial pressures on demand from the industry due to the financial crisis. Second, regional natural gas markets are increasingly interlinked. The various regional markets used to be more independent from each other, however, with the creation of numerous new LNG routes due to the emergence of that technology, regional markets are better interlinked.

Note however the divergence in prices between US and European gas prices since 2009. The diverging trends between the US and European natural gas prices is mainly due to the production of unconventional gas resources in the US, e.g.: shale gas, while this exploitation is often limited in Europe because of environmental concerns (e.g. France). The diverging trend is an indicator that the export capacity is insufficient (for now) in the US for the market prices to converge totally. In fact, before the emergence of the shale gas industry in the US, many LNG import stations have been built in prediction of a large shortfall in the natural gas production in the US. These stations cannot be used for export unless extensive transformation is taking place, which means that divergence in natural gas prices between the US and Europe will be possible until appropriate trade facilities are put in place. Nonetheless, regional natural gas price patterns are likely to converge even more in the future and that regional shocks will be short-lived as natural gas can be supplied from or to another region.

Thirdly, long-term natural gas delivery contracts are often linked to the evolution of oil prices (IEA 2009) explaining the close link between the prices of the two resources. Lastly, the availability of substitutes to natural gas in the end-market impacts the natural gas price evolution, limiting the amplitude of shocks on natural gas prices.

More than oil, natural gas is used to generate electricity and the cost of fuel accounts for the big part of its levelized cost of electricity (over 60 %). Due to this high share, gas-fired power plants are the most sensitive to fuel price variation, even more so than coal. Therefore, it is especially important for the investor to properly estimate the cost of natural gas over the lifetime of the power plant in order to get proper estimates for the cost per kWh. The variations in natural gas prices make such estimates impossible. Instead, investors use a steady fuel cost increasing rate based on what the theory predicts. [1]

During the production process in many production cases, the decision for using the level of input and supply of output is risky. Some inputs are negatively correlated with the variance of the output. For example, investment in the global warming reduction and improving environmental condition is negatively related to the variance of fossil fuel production. Some other inputs have positive relationship such as investing in high technology will improve the quality and the output variation of high technology products. [2]

the concept of risk in the production theory is studied mainly from two aspects: First, uncertainty arises from changes in the price of output and second, uncertainty arises from the volume of output. The latter is often referred to as the production risk, in which it can be explained by the inputs used in the production. The quantity of inputs that determine the output volume also influences the degree of output inconsistency or variability. For example, in the financial sector the interest rates and in the agriculture sector the use of fertilizer and

---

[1] Patrick A. Narbel • Jan Petter Hansen Jan R. Lien: Energy Technologies and Economics. Springer International Publishing Switzerland 2014. P 95: 97
[2] Nabaz T. Khayyat: Energy Demand in Industry. Springer Science+Business Media Dordrecht 2015. P 53

pesticides might be risky leading to increase in the variation of the output, while technology and labor might decrease the output risk. Other risks might increase or decrease the output. For example, currency risk in the financial sector, which is related to the risk that changes in the rate of foreign exchange will positively or negatively affect the value of the asset held in that currency. [1]

2.5.1. Supply Cost Curves

Although various organizations publish estimates of reserves and resources, it is challenging to categorize these definitions under a consistent classification system.

The respective organizations tend to report their quantities using different terms,

---

[1] Nabaz T. Khayyat: Energy Demand in Industry. Springer Science+Business Media Dordrecht 2015. P 53: 54

Table 1 Conventional and unconventional oil production costs for 2009 and 2030 in USD/BOE

	Production costs (2009)[a]			Production costs (2030)[c]	
Cost category	Lower bound (USD/BOE)	Upper bound (USD/BOE)	Technology change in %/year[b]	Lower bound (USD/BOE)	Upper bound (USD/BOE)
Oil and NGL					
CI	3.00	7.00	1.50	2.20	5.10
CII	7.00	13.00	1.50	5.10	9.45
CIII	13.00	20.00	1.00	10.55	16.20
CIV	20.00	29.00	0.50	18.00	26.10
CV	29.00	35.00	0.50	26.10	31.50
Heavy oil[d]		35.00	0.50		31.50
Oil sands		50.00	0.50		45.00
Shale oil		60.00	0.50		55.00

Table 2 Conventional and unconventional gas production costs for 2009 and 2030 in USD/MCF

	Production costs (2009)[a]			Production costs (2030)[c]	
Cost category	Lower bound (USD/MCF)	Upper bound (USD/MCF)	Technology change in %/year[b]	Lower bound (USD/MCF)	Upper bound (USD/MCF)
Natural gas					
CI	0.50	0.90	1.50	0.35	0.65
CII	0.90	1.40	1.50	0.65	1.00
CIII	1.40	2.30	1.50	1.00	1.65
CIV	2.30	3.10	1.00	1.85	2.50
CV	3.10	3.75	1.00	2.50	3.00
CBM[d]		3.75	1.00		3.00
Tight gas		4.00	1.00		3.25
Shale gas		5.00	1.00		4.00

concepts, and boundaries. Attempts to create universal resource classification systems have been undertaken by SPE/WPC/AAPG/SPEE (2007) and UNFC (2009). In the present study, conventional oil and gas volumes are distinguished on the basis of five production cost categories.

The first category (CI) represents favorable production conditions such as shallow reservoirs with high-quality oil. The standard definition of proved reserves (P90; 1P), for instance, falls under CI. This category often serves as a public policy tool for many economic, political, technical, and environmental considerations. Countries often utilize proved reserves to gain leverage in foreign policy, to design economic plans, and to form regulatory, market, and climate policies. The reason is that the proved reserve definition represents quantities that are recoverable under existing prices and technologies. Its use for long-term investment decisions or policy analyses is thus restricted.

The second category (CII) represents quantities that may be currently undiscovered but have a reasonable probability of being found. Probable reserves (P50; 2P) belong to CII. In time, these volumes will presumably come online as exploration and production efforts expand. As CI oil and gas is exhausted, CII will replace them and move into the CI category themselves.

Quantities that fall under the third category (CIII) are of a more speculative nature in terms of geological information and economic feasibility. Possible reserves (P10; 3P) fall under CIII. Over the medium to long term, as the CI and CII categories begin to dwindle, market and technological conditions should shift the CIII volumes into the CII and CI categories.

Categories CI to CIII represent conventional oil and gas volumes that can be delineated with current geological techniques. The main characteristic of these categories is the uncertainty associated with their eventual discovery. The fourth and fifth categories encompass increasing uncertainty with respect to economic, geological, technical, and environmental factors.

The possibilities of enhanced oil and gas recovery through tertiary production methods are classified as CIV and, however, may also apply to CI–CIII. Additions to reserves due to increased recovery factors from advanced technologies (e.g., steam injection, the use of solvents, chemical methods, CCS) are included in the CIV category.

Oil and gas located in deep offshore reservoirs falls under the fifth category (CV). These quantities cannot usually be produced with traditional methods because of technical and economic limitations. Some assessments may even consider CV quantities as "unconventional" due to the novelty of deep sea drilling, even though the hydrocarbon itself is "conventional" by geological definitions.

Supply cost curves are a function of remaining oil and gas volumes, production costs, and technological change. Table 1 shows the current oil production costs per BOE in 2009 USD, the assumed annual rates of technological improvement per production cost category, and the projected production costs for 2030. There are five assumed conventional oil cost categories with a lower and upper bound for each category. The assumed rates of technological improvement, ranging from 0.50 % to 1.50 % per year, reflect the observed fact that advancement is greater under favorable production conditions.

Applying an assumed rate is based on recent approaches to modeling technological change that capture the effect of progress occurring exogenously over time. For example, Nordhaus (2009) argues that there is a constant rate of exogenous technological change associated with time. In highest cost category (CV), for instance, compounded technological advancement of 0.50 % per year until 2030 reduces the upper bound from 35.00 to 31.50 USD/BOE. Annual productivity gains in the upstream oil and gas sectors have historically been observed at an average of about 1 %. However, periods of two-digit growth (usually in the short run) have often been followed by zero or negative increases, making productivity estimates highly uncertain. Thus, our projected rates may prove to be pessimistic or optimistic, "the most important variable in the long run is the least predictable: technical progress both in supply and in utilization."

Table 2 presents 2009 and 2030 gas production costs in USD per MCF, as well as technological improvement rates. In this case, technological advancement is assumed to range from 1.00 % to 1.50 % per year. The upper bound of the fifth cost category, CV, has decreased from 3.75 USD/MCF in 2009 to 3.00 USD/MCF in 2030, assuming compounded technological change of 1.00 % per year. It is important to note that the assumed rates of technological progress will not occur automatically over time. Rather, significant investments will be necessary to allow for productivity gains. Reduced interest rates should lead to increased investment in oil and gas projects, particularly those with a high proportion of capital costs.

Considering our time horizon (to 2030), the eventual result would be increased production and cost reductions due to technological learning. Conversely, an increase in interest rates will discourage investment, leading to reduced future supply and augmented prices and costs. For a detailed analysis on the relationship between interest rates and supply curves, refer to Bauer et al. (2008).

Applying the cost ranges of the five categories to the earlier-reported conventional oil and gas volumes in a fixed proportion leads to estimated oil and gas supply cost curves for Europe. Based on Aguilera et al. (2009), the proportion of conventional oil volumes across categories is assumed to be 5 % (CI), 15 % (CII), 60 % (CIII), 17.5 % (CIV), and 2.5 % (CV); for conventional gas, it is 30 % (CI), 47.5 % (CII), 15 % (CIII), 5 % (CIV), and 2.5 % (CV). In order to provide a greater level of detail, each cost category has been broken up into additional categories. These subcategories are created by evenly dividing the costs into five classes. For example, the subcategories for CI (oil) in USD/BOE are as follows: 3.00–3.80, 3.80–4.60, 4.60–5.40, 5.40–6.20, and 6.20–7.00.

The lower portions of Tables 1 and 2 show single production cost estimates for each of the unconventional sources. The 2009 estimates are simplistically based on the ranges presented in the oil and gas supply curves of IEA (2008, 2009, 2012).

Shale oil and shale gas are the most expensive, though still less than market oil and gas prices. Technological progress is also assumed to benefit the costs of unconventional production in 2030 at the same rates as category CV.

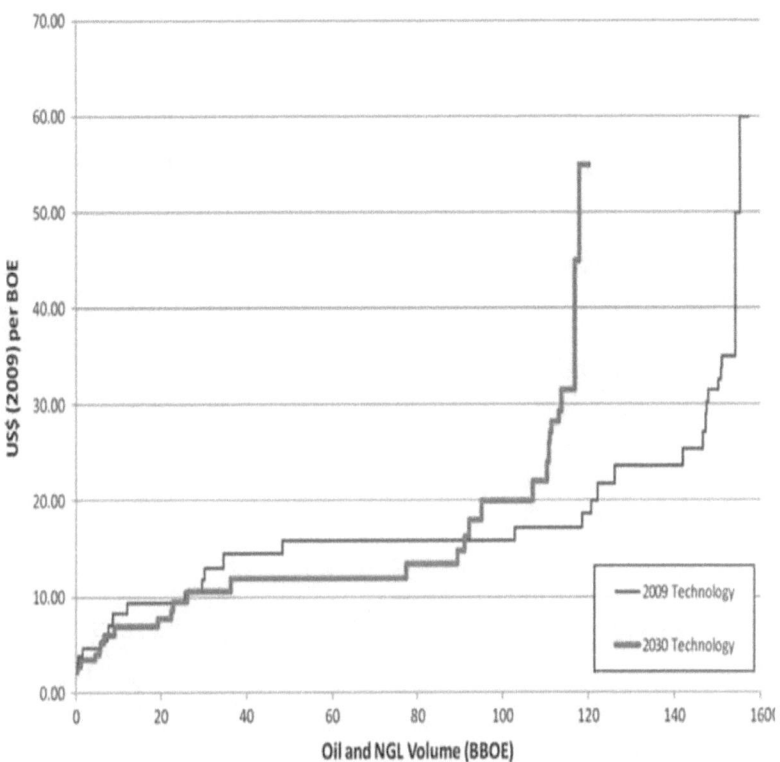

The Figure shows two oil supply curves—one for the volumes based on performance, productivity, and costs associated with 2009 technology and one for the volumes, performance, and production technology expected by 2030. The 2030 curves reflect production cost reductions due to technological advances over the period. However, the volumes in 2030 exclude any potential enhancement to the accessible oil resource base made possible by technological change and different market conditions but reflect the oil produced between 2009 and 2030 (assuming constant 2009 production levels). In any case, the estimated volume for 2009 already includes the oil from previously unassessed provinces as well as reserve growth.

The Figure follows the same procedure but presents supply curves for conventional gas.

The potential conventional and unconventional oil volume assessed for 2009 amounts to some 158 BBOE. This is calculated by subtracting European cumulative oil production until 2009, 57 BBOE (British Petroleum 2010), from the VSD-calculated conventional endowment plus the GEA-estimated unconventional endowment (215 BBOE). As defined above, endowment includes cumulative production, so cumulative oil production must be subtracted from the endowment in order to give the remaining volume. Assuming a constant oil production rate of 1.7 BBOE per year from 2009 to 2030 (British Petroleum 2010), the remaining total decreases to 120 BBOE in 2030.

For the case of conventional and unconventional gas, the total remaining volume in 2009 amounts to 4,378 TCF. This is equal to the VSD-calculated conventional total plus the

GEA-estimated unconventional total (4,688 TCF) minus cumulative

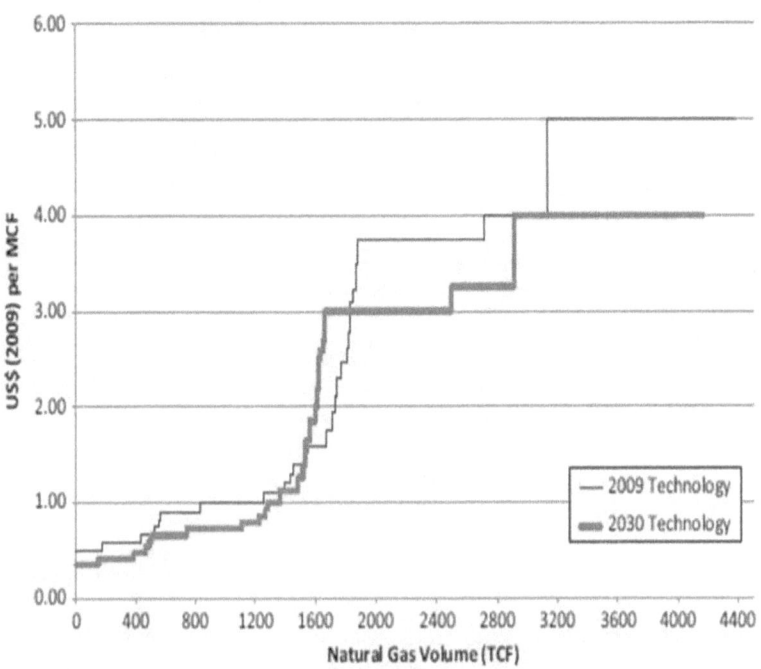

gas production until 2009 (310 TCF). A constant production rate of 9.8 TCF per year (British Petroleum 2010) is used to derive the volume in the 2030 supply curve, 4,162 TCF. [1]

2.6. Petroleum Price Reforms in china

Petroleum price regulation has experienced four stages. Pre-1981, petroleum prices were fully state-controlled. From 1981 to

[1] Walter Leal Filho • Vlasios Voudouris: Global Energy Policy and Security. Springer-Verlag London 2013. P 147: 152

1994, a 'dual track' pricing system was adopted, while from 1994 to 1998 petroleum prices were market-meditated. After 1998, domestic petroleum prices have been set by NDRC in accordance with the international energy market price (Hang and Tu 2007). Meanwhile, central government sets the regional prices of refined oil products according to the Singaporean oil market and as a result, the 1998 reform sees domestic oil prices closely following international prices. [1]

---

[1] Hengyun Ma 1 Les Oxley: China's Energy Economy. Springer-Verlag Berlin Heidelberg 2012. P 133

3. Petroleum market
3.1. WORLD SUPPLY STRUCTURE

Another aspect of oil movements concerns the pinpointing of canals via which the crude, produced in various nations, reaches its final markets and how much of this crude contributes to support the dynamics of the oil market through commercial transactions. In the first place we should split world production into two distinct segments:

_ that of the *guaranteed flows*, namely the part of world production that, every day, independently of the price level, is able to reach its final destination. This part represents about 88% of the production; and

_ that of the *flows dependent on the price*, namely that part of the production that reaches any final market whatsoever only if its price is adequate and competitive. This part represents about 12% of the production.

It is interesting to look into the two segments defined above and shown in the Figures, especially the one of the guaranteed flows, to understand the level of fragility of the physical markets for crude, where only a tiny fraction of the production is exchanged every day.

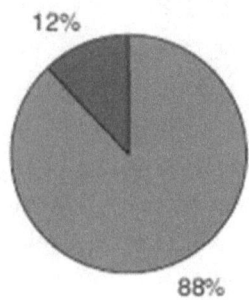

Therefore, in the oil market a gigantic space for manipulation is created. By moving only marginal quantities an enormous pressure can be exerted on the balance of the world market (such as the phenomenon of the squeeze on Brent).

_ About 55% of the crude extracted by the producing countries is used in their internal refining system to cover their domestic needs. A small percentage of refined products (under 10%), in excess of the domestic requirement, is exported to other markets.

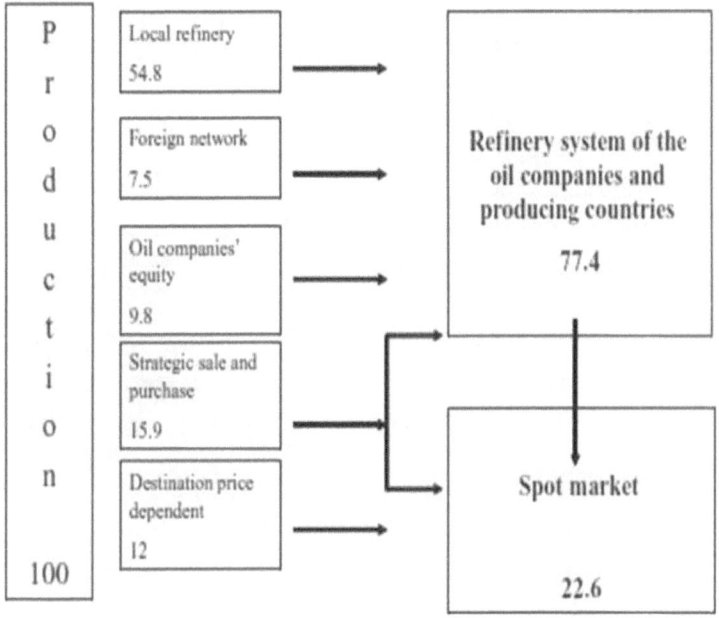

_ About 7–8% of the crude is transferred to refining and distribution circuits that some producing countries own in the main areas of consumption (e.g. Saudi Arabia, Venezuela, Kuwait, Libya).

_ About 10% represents the crude due to the oil companies for the repayment of their investments (the so-called equity quota) and which is sent either to their refining system or sold in the international markets.

_ Some 15–16% of the production, historically, is destined by many countries to repay works and goods of strategic nature (e.g. major civil works, infrastructures and means of transport, military expenses).

Only 12% of world production is linked every day to spot or short-term sales contracts. This segment, plus other fractions of crude from the preceding segments, for a total never greater than 25%, constitutes the base of what we call the physical oil market. Out of a production of around 88 million barrels per day, the crude responding to commercial transactions does not exceed 20–25 million barrels per day.

From these data it is easy to see how the market forces do not affect the overall mass of demand and world oil supply but only a very limited segment in the hands of just a few operators. This fragile and critical balance is rocked today by the power of speculative finance which upsets the precarious equilibrium of what was formerly the international oil market. [1]

3.1.1. Structure of Oil Industry

Before World War I, the world oil market was dominated by four major international oil companies: Shell, Standard Oil, Nobel, and Rothschild. The latter two companies were in Russia and were liquidated as private companies by the 1917 Russian Revolution. Another major company, founded by the British

---

[1] Salvatore Carollo: Understanding Oil Prices A John Wiley & Sons, Ltd., Publication. 2012. P 70:72

government, was the Anglo-Persian Company (now British Petroleum). In the 1920s, the oil market was essentially controlled by these three companies. In the 1930s, new major oil companies developed as offshoots of the old Standard Oil Company. They were Gulf, Texaco, Standard of California, Sohio, and Mobil. With these new entrants, the degree of competition in the world oil market increased, but only to a certain extent. In the 1940s and 1950s, the seven sisters (Gulf, Texaco, Standard of California, Sohio, Mobil, British Petroleum, Shell) had balanced the supply and demand mainly by market-sharing and joint producing agreements. To some extent these agreements distorted world market competition, resulting in an oligopoly market structure characterized by substantial differences between production cost and market price.

The deviation of oil prices from production costs allowed for vertical integration and controlling the market all the way from exploration to marketing. The share of the major oil companies in world oil production refining and marketing was about 60 percent. This concentration ratio, which indicates the degree of competition in the world oil market, has declined dramatically, especially in the production sector. This is due to the increased participation of oil-producing countries in production and to the evolution of the national oil companies. Table 2.5 shows the shares of the largest seven international oil companies in different sectors of the oil industry over the last three decades. It is clear that the market power of the majors has reduced,

Shares of the Largest International Oil Companies in Oil Industry Activities (Thousand Barrels per Day), 1990–2010

Company Activity	1990	% of World	2000	% of World	2010	% of World
BP						
Crude oil reserves[a]	7,313	0.26	6,508	0.20	5,559	0.14
Crude oil product	2,104	3.56	1,928	2.93	2,374	3.40
Crude oil processed	2,783	4.39	2,928	4.04	2,426	2.95
Refined products sold	3,837	5.77	5,859	7.65	5,927	6.82
ExxonMobil						
Crude oil reserves[a]	10,181	0.37	12,171	0.36	11,673	0.29
Crude oil product	2,491	4.22	2,553	3.88	2,422	3.47
Crude oil processed	4,952	7.80	5,692	7.79	5,253	6.38
Refined products sold	7,283	10.94	7,993	10.44	6,414	7.40
Total						
Crude oil reserves[a]	2,731	0.10	6,960	0.21	5,987	0.15
Crude oil product	411	0.69	1,433	2.17	1,340	1.92
Crude oil processed	832	1.31	2,411	3.33	2,009	2.44
Refined products sold	1,487	2.23	3,695	4.83	3,776	4.34
Royal Dutch/Shell						
Crude oil reserves[a]	10,107	0.37	6,907	0.21	5,179	0.13
Crude oil product	1,820	3.10	2,274	3.45	1,619	2.32
Crude oil processed	3,218	5.17	2,923	4.03	3,197	3.88
Refined products sold	4,962	7.46	5,574	7.28	6,460	7.43
Chevron						
Crude oil reserves[a]	5,909	0.21	8,519	0.25	4,270	0.10
Crude oil product	1,745	2.95	1,997	3.03	1,923	2.75
Crude oil processed	3,285	5.19	2,540	3.51	1,894	2.30
Refined products sold	4,680	7.03	5,188	6.78	3,113	3.58
Total Majors						
Crude oil reserves[a]	36,241	1.31	41,065	1.23	32,668	0.80
Crude oil product	8,571	14.51	10,185	15.46	9,678	13.85
Crude oil processed	15,070	23.79	16,494	22.70	14,779	17.96
Refined products sold	21,961	33.00	28,309	40.00	25,690	29.56
Total World						
Crude oil reserves[a]	2,759,106	100.0	3,330,425	100.0	4,076,000	100.0
Crude oil product	59,077	100.0	65,863	100.0	69,840	100.0
Crude oil processed	63,336	100.0	72,439	100.0	82,305	100.0
Refined products sold	66,539	100.0	76,537	100.0	86,900	100.0

yet they still control around 25 percent of world oil refining and about 35 percent of marketing activity.

Oil producers' participation in the oil industry began in 1960 when OPEC was established. OPEC was formed by five major oil-exporting countries: Iran, Iraq, Kuwait, Saudi Arabia, and Venezuela. Qatar joined in 1961 and was followed by Indonesia and Libya in 1962. By 1979, the number of OPEC members totaled 13, including the United Arab Emirates which joined in 1967, Algeria in 1969, Nigeria in 1971, Ecuador in 1973, and Gabon in 1975. From December 1992 to October 2007, Ecuador suspended its memberships, while Gabon terminated its membership in 1995. By January 2009, Indonesia suspended its membership, and Angola joined in the same year. Currently, OPEC has a total of 12-member countries.

In the 1960s, several national oil companies of the producing nations were established, although in most cases without significant market power. However, in the 1970s to 1990s, national oil companies gained more power over the oil industry and extended even more to refining and marketing. [1]

---

[1]Hussein K. Abdel-Aal, Mohammed A. Alsahlawi: Petroleum Economics and Engineering. Third Edition. Taylor & Francis Group, LLC. 2014. P 31:33

3.1.2. Structure of the Gas Industry

Natural gas is a mixture of hydrocarbon gases with almost 85 percent methane. It comes from oil wells as associated gas and non-associated when it is produced from gas wells. Before transporting natural gas to consumers, it has to be processed to separate all included hydrocarbons and obtain pure methane or dry gas.

For its economic and environmental advantages, natural gas has gained preference, and its share in the energy mix has been increasing since the 1980s. Consumption of natural gas has increased by more than 2 percent a year over the last 30 years. Since 2009, world demand for natural gas has declined as a result of the global economic crisis, but the supply of natural gas has increased due to capacity growth of liquefied natural gas (LNG) and new development of unconventional gases such as shale gas, especially in the United States.

As the global LNG demand dropped substantially, the supply of LNG improved as new LNG liquefaction plants opened in Qatar, Yemen, Indonesia, and Russia. During 2009 to 2016, approximately 233.5 million tons per annum (MMTPA) of new LNG liquefaction capacity are expected to come on-stream. The major contributors to this increase are Australia,

Natural Gas and LNG Exports and Imports (Billion cm), 2008

Country	Natural Gas Exports	Natural Gas Imports	LNG Exports	LNG Imports
Natural Gas Producers				
Russia	195	—	—	—
Canada	103	—	—	—
Norway	96	—	—	—
Netherlands	62	—	—	—
Qatar	58	—	39	—
Algeria	57	—	20	—
Turkmenistan	54	—	—	—
Indonesia	37	—	28	—
Malaysia	28	—	31	—
United States	28	—	—	—
Natural Gas Consumers				
United States	—	113	—	10
Japan	—	95	—	95
Germany	—	92	—	—
Italy	—	77	—	—
Ukraine	—	53	—	—
France	—	48	—	10
Spain	—	39	—	28
United Kingdom	—	37	—	—
Turkey	—	37	—	5
Korea	—	37	—	37

Source: Natural Gas Information, International Energy Agency (IEA), Paris, 2009. With permission.

Iran, Nigeria, and Qatar. The excess of natural gas supplies in the world has led LNG spot prices to hit new lows. The drop-in spot LNG prices has made buyers rethink long-term LNG contracts. Importers can now easily tap the global market for spot cargoes at lower prices than the long-term supply agreements.

The Table shows natural gas and LNG exports and imports by leading natural gas producers and consumers in 2008. The United States and Russia are the leading countries in natural gas production and consumption, while Japan and Korea the major importers of LNG.

In the United States, the gas industry has been regulated since the beginning of gas discovery. From time to time, such regulation created a supply shortage. However, in competitive markets, the price of natural gas reflects the interaction between the demand and supply, which are inelastic with respect to price in the short run. This market structure was enhanced by

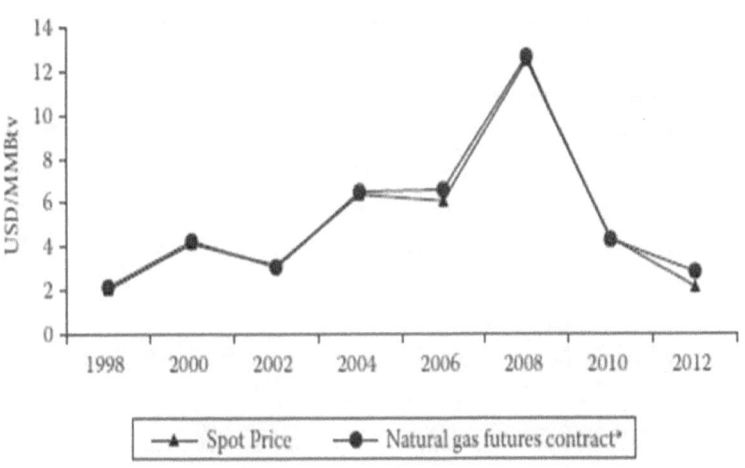

the drop in natural gas prices because of the decline in demand for natural gas as a result of the 1970s energy crisis and energy conservation policies. This allowed for direct deals between suppliers and buyers, which opened the door for natural gas spot markets. With more fluctuations in natural gas prices, the futures market for natural gas has developed. The New York Mercantile Exchange (NYMEX) became the trading floor for short- and long-term futures contracts. Spot prices reflect market conditions where prices for the contracts are based on delivery at the Henry Hub in Louisiana. The Figure presents natural gas spot prices and short-term futures contracts.

Natural gas prices outside the United States are basically linked to oil prices through long-term contracts. In the United Kingdom, the market is liberalized and subject to arbitrage between spot gas traded on the national balancing point (NBP) and continental European long-term contracts. In the continental European market, gas contracts are based on oil products prices. For Asia, natural gas prices are based on government-regulated levels with spot pricing for LNG. There are price differentials between these natural gas markets attributed to different market conditions and price formation whether spot prices or long-term gas contracts are related to oil prices. The financial crisis of 2008 caused a fall in spot gas prices as a result of a drop-in gas consumption. The two major spot markets,

Henry Hub and NBP, recorded lows at ranges of $3.5/MBTU and $4/MBTU, respectively, between 2009 and 2012. [1]

3.2. Oil Marketing

Marketing is the most complex sector of the world oil industry. Oil marketing may be viewed in many ways, including wholesale markets, in which large sales are made to sellers of small volumes, and versus retail markets, which sell to final consumers. Sometimes sales are on a spot or single-sale basis and sometimes on short- or long-term contracts. There are also differences between crude oil and oil product markets.

Historically, until the early 1970s, crude oil was marketed through integrated company systems. Sometimes producing/refining companies would exchange oil, usually on a barrel-for-barrel basis. Some crude oil, around 5 percent, was sold by producers through spot markets to refiners. This situation is now changed. Most of the world's equity crude has disappeared from the market, largely as a result of nationalization of the assets of most major oil producers. Although the traditional concessionary companies have retained preferred access to crude oil through service contracts, the amount of oil traded on a

[1] Hussein K. Abdel-Aal, Mohammed A. Alsahlawi: Petroleum Economics and Engineering. Third Edition. Taylor & Francis Group, LLC. 2014. P 36:39

spot basis has increased to above 50 percent. This trend has been accentuated by the development of formal oil exchange markets such as New York, London, Hong Kong, and Dubai. In recent years oil exchange markets allow for movement away from physical crude oil markets to paper markets which consist of futures options and forwards. Such movement has increased market speculation and price volatility rather than the fundamentals of the supply and demand forces.

Marketing was relatively simple for oil products in the past. There were essentially three main products: motor gasoline, heating oil, and heavy oil. Motor gasoline markets were, and remain, the most fragmented among the world's oil products. In the United States, which consumes about half of the world's gasoline supply, private service stations tend to be the main marketing distributors. In the rest of the world, major private or government companies own the outlets. However, company- or government-owned service stations tend not to compete on a price basis, but on advertising and locational advantages.

For the middle distillates, mainly heating oil, diesel fuel, and aviation jet fuel, the situation is more complex. For heating oil, competition is less among suppliers, which implies less emphasis on advertising and brand identification. Diesel fuel sale, however, is mostly for trucks and other heavy equipment such as railroad engines, construction equipment, and marine diesel engines. Because sales tend to be in larger volume than for motor gasoline, marketing relies on price differentials. Aviation fuel tends to be an especially profitable marketing area. This is due to the large volume involved and requirements for high-quality product.

Heavy fuel oil is mainly used for electric power generation. It is always sold on a wholesale basis, often under long-term contracts, with prices related to the prices of coal and natural gas.

Oil product pricing generally depends on crude oil price and the quality of crude in terms of sulfur content and density. The high quality of crude yields higher-value products which increases the refinery margins given the refinery process and configuration. However, beyond supply and demand, product pricing is affected by the degree of market competition, the way oil products are traded in the financial markets, and the governments' regulations. [1]

---

[1]Hussein K. Abdel-Aal, Mohammed A. Alsahlawi: Petroleum Economics and Engineering. Third Edition. Taylor & Francis Group, LLC. 2014. P 30:31

3.3. The Effect of the Relationship Between Oil Price and Stock Markets in Energy Sustainable Countries

Researchers have been attracted to the relation between the oil prices and the stock market indices that are the best indicator of the economic growth because of the data with high frequency. In the studies, whether the country analyzed is developed or developing had been an important factor. [1]

The results on developed countries are not fully consistent. Jones and Kaul (1996) measure how the stock prices are affected by the oil prices in the US, Canada, Britain, and Japan. They conclude that the stock prices react seriously to the oil price changes in Japan and Britain, while the reaction in the US and Canada is due to the future cash flow changes for the firms. On the other hand, Kilian and Vega (2011) do not find a significant relationship between oil price shocks and stock returns for some developed countries. Particularly Apergis and Miller (2009) analyzes eight developed countries and claims that international stock market returns do not respond in a large way to oil market shocks.

---

[1] Andre' Dorsman • O" zg€ur Arslan-Ayaydin • Mehmet Baha Karan: Energy and Finance. Springer International Publishing Switzerland 2016. P 130

The works for emerging economies provided conflicting results as well. Maghyereh (2004) finds that during the period of 1998–2004 the emerging economies don't show a significant reaction to oil price changes. He argues that oil price is an overvalued factor for the stock markets in emerging economies. However, Basher and Sadorsky (2006) come up with different results. In their research covering the period 1992–2005, oil is found as an important factor affecting the stock markets of emerging economies. [1]

Also, literature regarding the evolving nature of the relationship between oil prices and stock markets is reviewed. Although there is a common belief that oil prices have a negative correlation with the stock markets, this is not precisely the case anymore. As Kilian and Park (2009) state, oil price and stock market prices are affected by the same economic forces. Therefore, they might move in the same direction. Positive expectations for global economic growth, for instance move the oil prices and stock markets upward together. Moreover, crude oil is not only a commodity that is a significant input for the production, but it is a financial asset as D'ecclesia et al. (2014) mention. The dynamics behind the oil price and stock market returns are beyond the traditional

---

[1] Andre' Dorsman • O" zg€ur Arslan-Ayaydin • Mehmet Baha Karan: Energy and Finance. Springer International Publishing Switzerland 2016. P 130

demand and supply relation. Reboredo and Rivera-Castro (2014) state that before the 2008 financial crisis, oil prices do not have an effect on the stock market returns in Europe and the USA while positive interdependence is observed during the crisis period. Therefore, the nature of the relation between oil prices and stock markets is too complex and it is difficult to clarify briefly.

Oil exporter countries' stock markets differentiate regarding their reaction to oil price changes. Hammoudeh and Aleisa (2004) examine how the stock markets of Gulf States react to the oil price changes. They revealed that Saudi Arabia stock market index has the power to predict the oil prices. Maghyereh and Al-Kandari (2007) find a nonlinear relation between the stock market returns and oil prices in Bahrain, Kuwait, Oman and Saudi Arabia. Arouri et al. (2010) argue that the stock markets of Qatar, Oman, Saudi Arabia and UAE react to the oil shocks while the reaction of Bahrain and Kuwait was found statistically insignificant. [1]

As a brief, the studies analyzing the relation between oil prices and stock markets are varied. How the energy sustainability affects the relation between the stock markets and oil prices has not been studied yet, and this study opens a

---

[1] Andre′ Dorsman • O¨ zg€ur Arslan-Ayaydin • Mehmet Baha Karan: Energy and Finance. Springer International Publishing Switzerland 2016. P 130: 131

new avenue in the literature. Moreover, it is almost no comparative study in literature for the relationship between oil price and stock market performance of the high energy sustainable and the low energy sustainable countries. The main hypothesis of the study is that "the economies of energy sustainable countries are more resistant to oil price changes". More clearly, we expect a very weak connection between oil prices and performance of stock markets for energy sustainable countries. The conflicting results of previous studies, particularly about developed countries that possess advanced energy markets in literature are supporting our argument. [1]

3.4. Global LNG Markets

LNG differs from piped gas as it can be transported across oceans in tankers so that it is not limited to regional markets. Work on turning gas to liquids for storage had begun as early as the 1820s, but it was not until the 1960s that any form of LNG market began to take form. Th e delay in developing a global natural gas industry was due to the costs and technology involved in transferring the commodity from one region of the globe to another. In gas form, natural gas was limited to transport by pipelines. But as a liquid, natural gas takes up just one six-hundredth of the volume of the commodity in its

---

[1]Andre′ Dorsman • Ö˙ zgЄur Arslan-Ayaydin • Mehmet Baha Karan: Energy and Finance. Springer International Publishing Switzerland 2016. P 131

gaseous form, making it a real possibility to transport larger volumes by tanker. Th e key was to have LNG facilities to liquefy the gas and then regasify it at the other end. Those facilities had to have the capability of keeping the gas at the extremely low temperature of −260 °F (−162 °C), and pipelines to transport it from its point of entry facility and point of exit at the other end. In the 1960s, LNG was transported for the first time from Algeria to Europe. Because of the costs involved in putting the infrastructure in place, the contracts for natural gas supplies were all long-term contracts. For Japan, the development of the LNG industry proved to be a boon. Th ere was no possibility of pipelines reaching Japan from gas fields, and the country was searching for cleaner forms of energy when its first LNG shipment arrived from the USA in 1969 China and India both began receiving LNG shipments later in the twenty-first century and had signed long-term contracts with Qatar as they saw their increasing energy consumptions growing.

Despite the advantages of using gas in producing energy, LNG shipped by tankers could not compete with gas transported by pipelines in the twentieth century. It was not until the twenty-first century that the costs of transporting LNG were brought down to levels that made it competitive with piped gas.

The force behind those innovations was Qatar, which had made discoveries of natural gas starting in 1971 that made it the world's third largest holder of gas reserves with 871.59 billion cubic feet (24.66 billion cubic meters) of natural gas in 2014. Unlike Russia and Iran—the largest and second largest depositories of gas—Qatar is not located in a region where it can construct pipelines to the lucrative markets of Europe and Asia. Th us, it focused on making the transport of LNG cost-efficient. It bought tankers twice the size of those previously used to transport more gas at a lower cost. With ExxonMobil funding research into the transport of LNG, the problem of making LNG competitive with other forms of energy was ultimately solved by expanding the transport operation at every level, making the volumes transported competitive with piped gas because of the scale on which the operation was done. By 2007, Qatar had become the world's largest exporter of LNG, which gave the small kingdom the world's highest per capita GNP.

The LNG revolution opened other possibilities. Gas could also be stored at freezing temperatures and sold on spot markets so that its price was more reflective of supply and demand than the natural gas sold under long-term contracts that were tied to the price of oil. [1]

---

[1] Thijs Van de Graaf • Benjamin K. Sovacool Arunabha Ghosh • Florian Kern • Michael T. Klare: The Palgrave Handbook of the International Political Economy of

LNG has represented, over the last decade, the key driver underpinning the progressive globalization of international gas markets. In fact, two of the three world's key gas markets (Europe and Asia) have become more and more interconnected due to inter-regional LNG trade. Th is situation might well expand in the future also to the third key gas market, North America, due to the entrance of US LNG into the global market.

LNG trade, which is projected to continue to grow strongly over the next decades, is also increasing the price links between the three regional markets through the potential for arbitrage. Th is section sheds light on the key developments of this important market.

Global LNG trade has constantly grown over the last decades. the volume of LNG trade expanded from less than 50 million tons per annum (Mtpa) in 1990 to more than 200 Mtpa in 2014.

Both, the number of LNG exporting and importing countries, have grown significantly, from about seven in 1990 to about 20 and 30 respectively in 2014. In 2014, Qatar was the key LNG exporter of the world (covering one-third of global LNG supply), followed by Malaysia, Australia, Nigeria,

Indonesia, Trinidad, Algeria, Russia and other minor suppliers.

Th e Middle East thus represents the leading LNG exporting region in the world. In the same year, Japan and South Korea imported more than half of global LNG (only Japan imported more than 30 percent), followed by China, India, Taiwan and several other minor importers. Asia and Asia Pacific markets, thus, represent the most important LNG importing region at global level, with a combined demand of 75 percent in 2014.

However, this figure is rapidly evolving, with the Chinese and the Indian markets expected to grow strongly over the next years. In perspective, LNG share of inter-regional trade is expected to further rise over the next decades. Th e IEA estimates that this share will grow from the current level of about 40–50 percent in 2040. LNG exports are set to rise mainly in Australia, Africa, North America and Russia. [1]

However, this favorable situation for LNG importers might well reverse in the 2020s, with a new cycle of tighter markets resulting from delayed investment in new LNG projects, due to low prices in the period 2015–2020. In fact, many greenfield LNG projects (thus

---

[1]Simone Tagliapietra: Energy Relations in the Euro-Mediterranean. 2017. P 62

expected to come online after 2020) are already being reconsidered all over the world from Africa to Australia, to North America. For instance, the prospects of a new wave of post-2020 Australian projects is being reconsidered after announcements of final investment decision postponements or even project cancellations from different international companies. Th e same phenomenon is also already appearing in Canada and in Russia.

To focus on the prospects for Europe in the period up to 2020, it is possible to expect that dropping LNG prices will strongly affect the overall structure of European gas markets. In fact, the availability of low-cost LNG will put pressure on gas producers such as Russia, Algeria and Norway, which will have to decide on whether to defend its existing pricing formulae or defend its market share by competing with LNG suppliers.

This is particularly true if considering that about 150 Bcm of gas import contracts to the EU are set to expire over the next ten years. However, it should be noted that among the three key pipeline gas suppliers to Europe, Russia enjoys the most resilient contracts for the next decade. In fact, Russia will still have 80 Bcm of minimum contracted quantity by 2025 (down from 100 Bcm today). On this basis, Russia is contractually well protected against a massive wave of LNG expected to materialize in the second half of the present decade. This is not the case with Algeria and Norway, which are much more exposed.

Having said this, Russia will most likely be committed to export to Europe, much more than the minimum contracted quantities, and for this reason, Gazprom has already announced that it will fight for market share in Europe. As a matter of fact, already over the last years, Russia has been selling its volumes above the minimum contracted quantities mainly at spot basis. Therefore, it is very possible to expect a future price war in Europe with LNG competing with Russian gas at spot basis. Th e case for such a development is also entailed in the fact that in Europe, over the last ten years, spot pricing increased from 15 percent to 60 percent on average. This ratio represents already 90 percent in North-western Europe, a region that represents 50 percent of European gas markets and where a competition between LNG and Russia gas is already in place. [1]

In 2012, Japan imported 87 million tons of LNG or 36.2% of total worldwide LNG imports of 239 million tons. The main sources, representing >70% of the total, are Asia-Pacific countries such as Australia, Malaysia, Russia, and Brunei.

---

[1] Simone Tagliapietra: Energy Relations in the Euro-Mediterranean. 2017. P 64: 65

LNG production is dispersed more widely around the world, making it less exposed to geopolitical risk than oil.

Caloric values of nearly all projects used to be 43–46 MJ/m^3. Since around the early 2000s, however, the number of projects producing LNG with relatively small caloric value (~41 MJ/m^3) has steadily increased. As a result, the volume of LPG required to adjust caloric value rose in Japan, so that several city gas suppliers lowered the standard caloric value of city gas to reduce the volume of LPG used. The caloric value of gas from unconventional sources now being developed (such as shale gas and coalbed methane) also tends to be low, from 40 MJ/m^3 or less to ~42 MJ/m^3.

The characteristics of LNG as a city gas resource are as follows. LNG is cooled and liquefied natural gas and under normal pressure has a very low temperature, approximately -160 C. The main component of LNG is methane, and its caloric value varies with its percentage of ethane, propane, butane, and others. Because it has the smallest C/H ratio of any fossil fuel, it produces the least CO_2 per unit caloric value when combusted. Because impurities such as sulfur and nitrogen content are removed during liquefaction, LNG produces the least NO_x and So_x emissions of any fossil fuel when combusted. However, special receiving terminals and gas facilities are required to handle very low-temperature LNG.

Given the importance of its low exposure to geopolitical risk and strong environmental friendliness, LNG is rated an "important energy source that will assume a growing role" in Japanese energy policy. [1]

Because LNG gas pricing for recent projects has been linked to the US Henry Hub price rather than JCC (Japanese Customs-Cleared Crude Oil), procurements from these projects are likely to increase because of the greater diversity of pricing mechanisms anticipated.

Advances must be made in LNG mixing technology to furnish the flexibility to receive the many types of LNG. Using simulations and actual testing on LNG tanks, the main challenges in the near future will be to clarify conditions required to mix LNG of variable densities in LNG tanks with various mixing capabilities and to enable mixing of LNG in LNG tanks without such capabilities. [2]

---

[1] Yukitaka Kato • Michihisa Koyama • Yasuhiro Fukushima • Takao Nakagaki: Energy Technology Roadmaps of Japan. Springer Japan 2016. P 199: 201
[2] Yukitaka Kato • Michihisa Koyama • Yasuhiro Fukushima • Takao Nakagaki: Energy Technology Roadmaps of Japan. Springer Japan 2016. P 213

Natural gas markets have historically operated as three distinct regional markets: North America, Asia, and Europe. In North America, the build-up of shale gas supplies in the period since 2008 led to a domestic supply glut that created downward pressure on prices and reversed trade flows significantly. US natural gas imports peaked in 2007 at 129 billion cubic meters (bcm) of pipeline gas and 21.6 bcm of LNG imports.6 A supply glut and reduced trade contributed to regional market dislocation and record spreads between the US Henry Hub price and major hubs in Europe and Asia from 2008 to 2015. [1]

China's imports of liquefied natural gas (LNG) hit a monthly record of 5.03 million tons in December, customs data showed, as purchases spiked to cover a surge in demand under Beijing's push to replace coal with gas for households and factories.

December shipments came in 24 per cent ahead of November's previous record of 4.056 million tons and were up 35 per cent from a year earlier, according to China's General Administration of Customs.

Full-year imports jumped 46 per cent compared with 2016 to record 38.13 million tons, according to the customs data, overtaking

---

[1] World Energy Resources. World Energy Council. 2016. P 10

South Korea as the world's second-largest buyer for the fuel after Japan.

Beijing's drive to heat millions of homes and power thousands of factories in northern China with gas has caused a spike in demand, leading companies to pull in cargoes from suppliers as diverse as Nigeria, Angola and Norway.

Meanwhile the data showed aviation fuel exports rose 7.9 per cent to record 1.69 million tons from December 2016 -- when the previous record of 1.57 million tons was set -- and 17 per cent from 1.45 million tons in November. [1]

3.5. Oil and Gas Accounting

Oil and gas accounting is somewhat different from the conventional accounting system with some specificities. Therefore, a short note on oil and gas accounting is presented in this section for the convenience of the readers.

Oil and gas accounting has evolved over the years to meet the unique nature of upstream business, diverse need, and atypical challenges of E&P sector. An E&P company deals with nonrenewable products and assets, which are associated with high risk, huge investment, and long gestation period. Oil and gas accounting relates to four basic costs,

[1] Al Hilal Publishing and Marketing Group. 2017

namely, acquisition cost (mining lease), exploration cost, development cost, and production cost. There are two methods of oil and gas accounting, namely, Successful Efforts Method and Full Cost Method. The basic differences between these two methods are related to capitalizing or expensing the incurred cost, and the size of the cost center over which costs are accumulated and amortized.

The cost center under *Successful Efforts Method* is a lease area, field, or reservoir and is much smaller than the cost center under Full Cost Method, which is generally a country.

Under Successful Efforts Method, a direct relationship is required between costs incurred and resources discovered. Consequently, only successful searching costs that directly result in the discovery of proven reserves are considered as the cost of finding oil or gas and are capitalized. The costs incurred in finding, acquiring, and developing reserves are typically capitalized on a field-by-field basis. The capitalized costs are allocated to commercially viable hydrocarbon reserves and are depleted on a field-by-field basis as production starts. The unsuccessful searching costs that do not result in an asset are expensed with. In summary, in Successful Efforts Method, the cost center is normally not larger than a field, and the acquisition and development costs are fully capitalized, and exploration cost is partly capitalized (drilling exploratory, appraisal, and test wells) and partly expensed (G&G, unproved properties, dry hole/well, etc.).

In contrast, *Full Cost Method* considers both successful and unsuccessful costs as capitalized, even though the unsuccessful costs have no future economic benefit. All costs incurred in searching, acquiring, and developing the reserves in a large geographic cost center or pool are capitalized. A cost center or pool is typically a country; the cost pools are then depleted on a country basis as production starts. If exploration efforts in the country or the geological formation are wholly unsuccessful, the costs are expensed with.

In short, in Full Cost Method, the cost center is typically not smaller than a country, and acquisition, development, and exploration costs are fully capitalized. [1]

3.6. The World Crude Oil Paradoxes

For some years now, the price of oil has been out of control. None of the great names of the industry, the production cycle or the oil market is able to intervene to decide its level or guide its progress. The oil companies, the OPEC producing countries as well as the non-OPEC,

---

[1]Sanjib Chowdhury: Optimization and Business Improvement Studies in Upstream Oil and Gas Industry. John Wiley & Sons, Inc. 2016. P 290:291

the consuming countries, the consumers: not one of these has this capability.

The price of oil, in the imagination of western consumers, is still linked to the equilibrium developed during the 1970s and 1980s, with the emerging of the Persian Gulf countries and the OPEC nations.

It is still a popular belief that the cartel of the largest oil producing countries in the world is capable of regulating the volume of production and using this key raw material to achieve political aims.

Even today, when the price of oil rises beyond any level considered critical, the vast majority of the oil market analysts turn their eyes towards Vienna, where the oil ministers of the OPEC countries meet, imagining, hoping for and analyzing decisions which either will not be taken or, if taken, will turn out to be completely ineffective. Lately, in some market reports, more sophisticated analyses are merely focused on the availability of OPEC countries' spare capacity; linking to this factor the dynamics of the oil price. When we look at the graph of the price of crude oil in Figure 1.1 we do not see the result of market forces, but rather a design traced by the hand of a powerful invisible architect who, following his own purposes, has established a course along which the price of oil should travel.

Since the end of 1998 analysts, oil companies and producing countries have mistaken every forecast of the price of oil, clearly showing not only that they no longer control the fundamental market mechanisms, but that they are not even able to comprehend its real dynamics – it is as if the invisible architect had lost his pencil.

If we take our memory back to December 1998, when the price of crude oil fell to $9 per barrel, all the respected names of the oil industry, bar none, forecast that the price would stay for at least one or two decades under $15 per barrel. It is enough to glance at the investment budgets of all the oil companies or the financial programs of the producing

countries to confirm that only the most optimistic among them estimated maximum price levels between $14 and $15 per barrel in the long run.

Some oil companies, based on this view, hedged their production at this level of prices and went bankrupt. Yet only a few months later, in the summer of 2000, the price had already reached $35 per barrel, taking everyone – market analysts, oil companies, producing countries, economists, politicians and consumers – by surprise. Rivers of ink were consumed to explain the nature of this event through analysis where the causes were sought in transient factors; a sudden storm, nervousness between two OPEC countries, political uncertainties and so on.

The years of the energy crises were far away and deeply buried in the collective subconscious. The reappearance of such a thorny question was regarded, before it raised any anxiety, as almost a nuisance. Still today, after a decade of price hikes for crude from $9 to more than $140 and then down to $37 and once again above $120 per barrel, most people limit themselves to reciting a series of clich´es to try to find justifications for an incomprehensible phenomenon:

_ Limited supply from the producing countries, apparently inadequate to satisfy the growing demand for oil.

_ Unexpected growth in the demand for oil by China and India, apparently upsetting the stability of the oil market.

_ Tensions in the Middle East.

_ The prospect of a decrease in the crude reserves/crude production ratio and therefore the availability of spare capacity.

_ The excessive taxes on petroleum products (gasoline, diesel, LPG etc.) imposed by European governments.

This type of analysis has the advantage of being simple and easily presentable to the public at large, without, however, explaining what has really happened or is happening. Nevertheless, this approach has enabled some commentators to exaggerate on the contentious issues regarding the excessive power of the OPEC countries and the ways to bring them to reason.

The problem which all serious analysts have to face up to is actually quite simple. The essence is to explain oil price movements by use of the classic model of economics, which assumes that price is a function of the relationship between demand and supply:

Price = f (demand, supply)

This principle of economics seems too valid to allow any space for querying it. Notwithstanding this, the fundamental classic method applied *tout-court* to the oil market does not work. Yes, it is correct to say that the price is linked to the supply and demand balance, but of which good? We need to find out the merchandise or commodity whose supply and demand is determining the dynamics of oil price. For sure, it is not the physical crude oil.

OPEC has programmed and put into effect increases or cuts in production on numerous occasions, but always with scarce results. To every public announcement of increased production by the OPEC countries, the markets have responded with an increase in the crude oil price by at least a couple of dollars per barrel – and vice versa when they announced cuts.

It is therefore reasonable to question whether the economic model utilized really works or if it is applied in an incorrect way to the oil market. Or, rather, that the technological complexity of this market does not allow it to be modelled on the simple relationship between demand and supply at a global level. The internal dynamics of this particular market require a much more detailed and complex model, capable of describing some of the fundamental dynamics of the system.

Unfortunately, the majority of analysts in this field have exclusively economic backgrounds and tend to apply general or econometric models to the crude oil, which are suitable for other commodities (coffee,

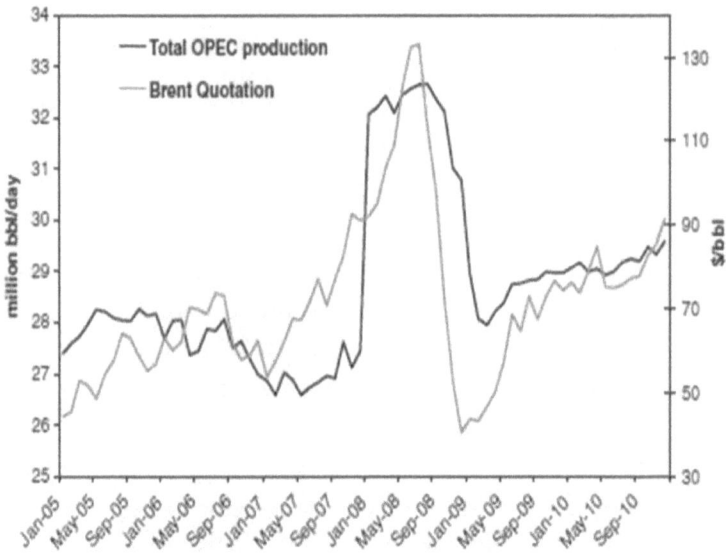

copy, gold etc.), where the production and technological transformation processes are less complex.

One starting point should be the recognition that what is commonly called the oil market is actually the conjunction and interaction of different markets which operate separately and independently but which are linked by certain complex forms of correlation and dynamics.

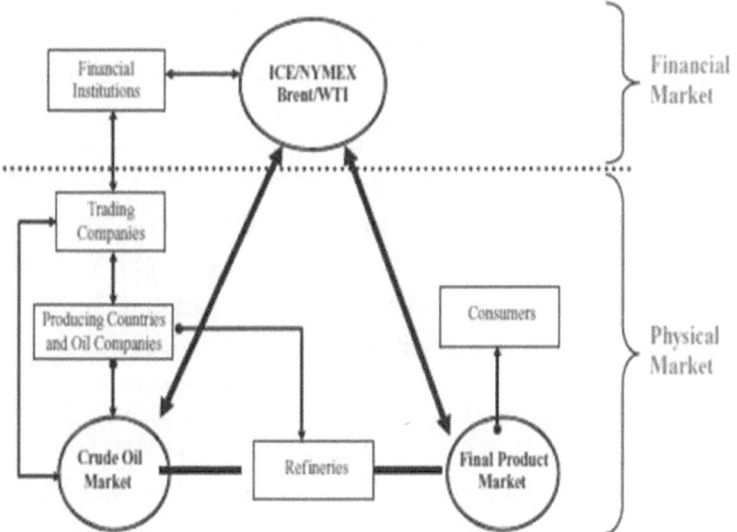

We refer now to the crude oil market (raw material), to the finished products market (gasoline, diesel, jet fuel, fuel oil, chemical feedstocks, lubricants) and to the financial market for crude and finished products (futures). We should always remember that in our cars and in airplanes we do not use crude oil, but finished products, which are increasingly difficult to produce. We cannot also neglect the dramatic developments of the futures market and its predominant role in the world economy.

Each and all these markets respond to different behavioral patterns and they are operated by bodies with differing interests, culture and business objectives. A model that does not take into account the interrelations between these markets and their individual dynamics is incapable of describing what happens to oil prices.

When the analyst is confronted by the unequivocal event of a price variation and having only the classic model of the global demand/ supply, he can only create a scenario of probable events (input to the model), which, when processed, might generate the variation in price which actually took place. If the price rises it is clear that there must have been an increase in demand or a reduction in supply. Therefore, one looks for all the clues which might prove that something like this has taken place. In the absence of reliable and prompt information there is more than enough space for these concoctions. It is thus very easy to reach the mistaken conclusion that China and India (the distant enemy, the invisible tartars) are becoming the critical factors for our planet. And that certainly OPEC (the conflict of civilizations) is yet again, for political and ideological reasons, not producing enough crude. Unquestionably there is no need to verify the production data of Venezuela under Chavez, or Iran under Ahmadinejad. It seems highly likely that both would wish to create problems for the west by raising prices.

The economic and strategic importance of the themes related to the price of crude oil would require a far more detailed technical analysis.

In this discussion we shall firstly try to examine the structural changes in the oil industry in recent decades, to see what has changed to make these dramatic and uncontrollable variations in price possible. And above all we shall try to understand why, in the space of a few short weeks (August–November 2008), without having seen even a small variation in the physical crude oil demand/supply situation the price tumbled from $144 to $37 per barrel. Then, in a couple of months it climbed back to $70–80 per barrel, exceeding again $120 per barrel in 2011.

These events have silenced many analysts, who have not been able to provide consistent answers to the following questions. First of all, why did the price drop in 2008? What happened in those few weeks? Did the

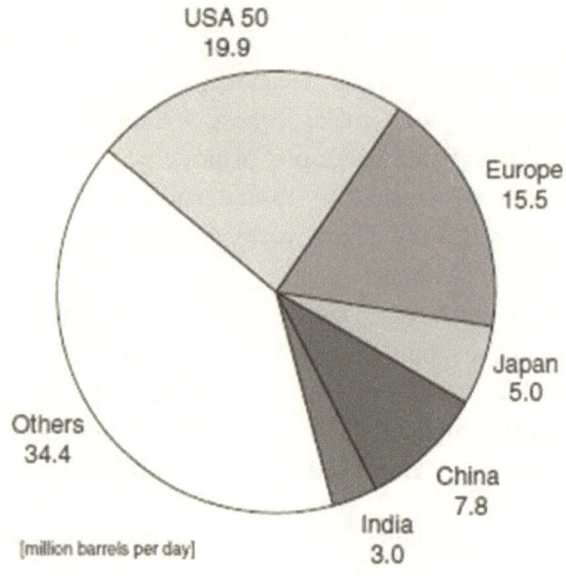

demands of China and India dry up or did the tensions in the Middle East calm down? Was OPEC flooding the markets with crude? The truth is that OPEC cut production, the data regarding world demand for oil (see Figure 1.4) showed no reduction in global consumption, and – in the previous weeks – the Middle East lived through one of the most dramatic crises in recent history. In all this turmoil, the oil price plunged by almost $110 per barrel.

What is the factor that then pushed the price up again above $120 per barrel, during a worldwide dramatic economic crisis and stagnation of oil consumption? [1]

---

[1] Salvatore Carollo: Understanding Oil Prices A John

3.7. Final market and export prices

A major challenge for governments in the taxation of export projects is ensuring that the price which is used for calculating the government take is a fair and reasonable one. The lack of other gas sales prices to benchmark against and the level of tariffs charged by the owners of the links in the chain between the export point and the price paid for the gas in the final market, makes this difficult.

In an LNG project, for example, the FoB price is commonly used for calculating tax in the midstream or integrated projects. This is supposed to be the price paid by the end user, net of deductions for the transportation, regasification and marketing of the gas. Both the final market price and the level of deductions significantly impacts the FoB value, so government has a strong motive to ensure that all of these are fair. This creates difficult challenges.

The first issue is establishing that the final market price compares with similar sales by other producers into similar markets. Most gas export sales are under long-term (20–30 years) contracts, and the terms of sales agreements reflect numerous factors. The gas price in any period is normally derived from a base price agreed at the time of signing the

---

Wiley & Sons, Ltd., Publication. 2012. P 1:6

contract and reflective of markets at the time, then linked by formulae which refer to the prevailing prices of competing fuels, inflation and other indices. Price floors and ceilings are often included.

Shifts in bargaining power and market conditions over time mean that the price being paid for gas under one agreement may be significantly different from that under another. These prices are also only rarely reported, so it is difficult to ascertain if the price in any particular contract is significantly higher or lower than is being paid for gas from other sources. In these situations, governments can refer to the few published gas prices that exist, with the most well-known being the Henry Hub spot price in the US. In Europe, the most established spot price index is the National Balancing Point (NBP) in the UK.

Where the final destination is expected to be a market which does have reported gas prices, the sales agreement will often take the reported price as the basis for the FoB price, less deductions and any additional indexation factors.

Thus, sales to the US could reference Henry Hub, with the FoB price increasing or decreasing as that price changes. The more directly the sales price is associated with a widely reported spot price, the more transparent the agreement can be seen to be and the more likely it is that the FoB price is fair.

The government of the producing country should also be concerned with the level of deductions being made from the final price to cover the costs of getting the gas to the market. An FOB price derived from the final market in the US, for example, might be expressed as follows:

FoB Price = Henry Hub Price × (100 − (A + B + C))% − (X + Y + Z), where

• A = volumes lost in liquefaction process.

• B = volumes lost in regasification process.

• C = volumes lost in pipeline to Henry Hub/market.

• X = shipping tariff from export point to receiving terminal.

• Y = tariff for regasification.

• Z = pipeline tariff from regasification plant to Henry Hub/market.

An array of factors influences the levels of tariffs which are charged by the owners of the shipping, regasification and pipeline links in the chain. These include the availability of alternative suppliers of the services and facilities, distances involved, operating and capital costs of the facilities and the rates of return included in the owners' tariff calculations (which may be regulated but normally are not).

The same companies may own more than one of these links and have an interest in moving economic rent to the lowest-taxed link. Thus, government needs to carefully monitor and benchmark each of the tariffs being deducted from the final sales price. Although this can be very difficult – and investors clearly have advantages of asymmetry of information – there is an increasing amount of data and methodologies in the public domain which can help establish benchmarks.

For example, third-party tanker freight rates are publicly quoted and several pipeline companies publish existing tariff rates on their websites.

Guidelines for 'reasonable' rates of return to be included in gas processing and pipeline tariffs are established under the US Federal Energy Regulatory Commission (FERC: www.ferc.gov) and Canada's National Energy Board (NEB: www.neb.gc.ca) rulings. It remains true, however, that ensuring fees charged for handling and processing gas (outside of the producing government's jurisdiction) are fair and reasonable is a significant problem for many governments.

One possible solution to this is to place the 'burden of proof' onto the producing company in a self-assessment of the FoB price received. Under this policy, the company would need to demonstrate to the government that the fees it was paying (and volume losses it incurs) are within a reasonable range for the relevant cargoes.

A final issue related to netback pricing which has emerged in recent years is that the agreed FoB price may not actually reflect the final realized price. Some companies have developed integrated LNG businesses and can make use of their presence in different markets to optimize the economic benefit from any LNG trade. For example, an LNG buyer could agree to pick up LNG cargoes from a producing country, with an agreed price formula linked to the prevailing Henry Hub gas price, with the intention that the cargoes will be sold into the US market. However, if the buyer has an opportunity to sell the cargo into a different market (e.g. Asia), then it can do so and benefit from the price upside. The producing government (and producing company) will receive none of the upside unless the LNG sales agreement specifically addresses the issue. As a result, producers are beginning to seek specific sharing mechanisms for additional price upside in new LNG agreements. [1]

---

[1] Philip Daniel, Michael Keen and Charles McPherson:

3.8. Revenue items

In most cases the revenues will be due to the sale of hydrocarbons. In determining these gross revenues, oil and/or gas prices must be assumed. The oil price forecast is often based on a flat real terms (RT) price (i.e. increasing in price at the forecast rate of inflation) or flat money of the day (MOD) price (i.e. price stays the same and is thus declining in RT). Both the level and method of price forecast are a matter of taste, and the industry analysts have in the past been notoriously poor at predicting oil price. Oil price is often linked to a regional marker crude such as Brent crude in the North Sea; the specific crude price is adjusted for specific conditions such as crude quality and geographic location. A gas price forecast may be indexed to the crude market price or be taken as the result of a negotiated price with an identified customer. A peculiarity of some gas contracts is that a fixed gas price is agreed for a very long period of time, possibly the lifetime of the field, which may result in disparities if the oil price and prevailing gas price change dramatically. Such contracts will often partially index gas price to the market price of the crude, and to other energy forms such as electricity prices. [1]

The Taxation of Petroleum and Minerals. international Monetary Fund. 2010. P 178: 180

([1])Frank Jahn, Mark Cook and Mark Graham: HYDROCARBON EXPLORATION AND PRODUCTION. 2ND EDITION. Elsevier B.V. 2008. P

References

1. Al Hilal Publishing and Marketing Group. 2017
2. Alastair Sweeny: Black Bonanza. John Wiley & Sons Canada, Ltd. 2010.
3. Andre′ Dorsman • O″ zgϵur Arslan-Ayaydin • Mehmet Baha Karan: Energy and Finance. Springer International Publishing Switzerland 2016.
4. Andy Lipow: Keeping the US crude oil exports flowing. Tank storage magazine. Volume 12, Issue 3.2016.
5. Bert Droste-Franke • Martin Carrier Matthias Kaiser • Miranda Schreurs Christoph Weber • Thomas Ziesemer: Improving Energy Decisions. Springer International Publishing Switzerland 2015.
6. Carl Larry: The new normal for the US oil industry. Tank storage magazine. Volume 1, Issue 1.2015.
7. data services dep. 2016
8. Enerdata : The energy mix remains overly carbon intensive despite the slight decrease of coal. 2017. P 2
9. Frank Jahn, Mark Cook and Mark Graham: HYDROCARBON EXPLORATION AND PRODUCTION. 2ND EDITION. Elsevier B.V. 2008.
10. Georgios M. Kopanos · Pei Liu Michael C. Georgiadis: Advances in Energy Systems

Engineering. Springer International Publishing Switzerland 2017.
11. Hengyun Ma 1 Les Oxley: China's Energy Economy. Springer-Verlag Berlin Heidelberg 2012.
12. http://www.opec.org/opec_web/en/index.htm
13. Hussein K. Abdel-Aal, Mohammed A. Alsahlawi: Petroleum Economics and Engineering. Third Edition. Taylor & Francis Group, LLC. 2014.
14. Iakovos Alhadeff: Energy & Terrorism Part 3. Free ebook.net 2016.
15. Investments in exploration/production and refining 2015. IFP Energies Nouvelles - January 2016.
16. James G. Speight: The Chemistry and Technology of Petroleum. FOURTH EDITION. Taylor & Francis Group, LLC. 2007.
17. Jinjun Xue • Zhongxiu Zhao • Yande Dai • Bo Wang: Green Low-Carbon Development in China. Springer International Publishing Switzerland 2013.
18. Keeping up with demand. Tank storage magazine. Volume 11, Issue 6.2015.
19. Leo Lester: Energy Relations and Policy Making in Asia. 2016.
20. Nabaz T. Khayyat: Energy Demand in Industry. Springer Science+Business Media Dordrecht 2015.

21. Naoyuki Yoshino • Farhad Taghizadeh-Hesary: Monetary Policy and the Oil Market. Asian Development Bank Institute 2016.
22. Nazim Muradov: Liberating Energy from Carbon: Introduction to Decarbonization. Springer Science+Business Media New York 2014.
23. Organization of the Petroleum Exporting Countries. Annual Report 2014.
24. Patrick A. Narbel • Jan Petter Hansen Jan R. Lien: Energy Technologies and Economics. Springer International Publishing Switzerland 2014.
25. Patrik Thollander • Jenny Palm: Improving Energy Efficiency in Industrial Energy Systems. Springer-Verlag London 2013.
26. Philip Daniel, Michael Keen and Charles McPherson: The Taxation of Petroleum and Minerals. international Monetary Fund. 2010.
27. PROF. DR. ENG H. FARAG/ ENG. A, ELMISSIRIEGUIDELINES FOR EVALUATION OF NATURAL GAS PROJECTS.
28. R.W. Bentley: Introduction to Peak Oil. Springer International Publishing Switzerland 2016.
29. Robert Ayres: ENERGY, COMPLEXITY AND WEALTH MAXIMIZATION. Springer International Publishing Switzerland 2016.

30. Roger Boyd: Energy and the Financial System Springer Cham Heidelberg New York Dordrecht London 2013.
31. Rossella Bardazzi • Maria Grazia Pazienza Alberto Tonini: European Energy and Climate Security. Springer International Publishing Switzerland 2016.
32. Salvatore Carollo: Understanding Oil Prices A John Wiley & Sons, Ltd., Publication. 2012.
33. Sanjib Chowdhury: Optimization and Business Improvement Studies in Upstream Oil and Gas Industry. John Wiley & Sons, Inc. 2016.
34. Sidney Borowitz: FAREWELL FOSSIL FUELS Reviewing America's. Energy Policy. Plenum Press, New York in 1999.
35. Simone Tagliapietra: Energy Relations in the Euro-Mediterranean. 2017.
36. Thijs Van de Graaf • Benjamin K. Sovacool Arunabha Ghosh • Florian Kern • Michael T. Klare: The Palgrave Handbook of the International Political Economy of Energy. 2016.
37. U.S. Energy Information Administration. Annual Energy Outlook 2015.
38. Walter Leal Filho • Vlasios Voudouris: Global Energy Policy and Security. Springer-Verlag London 2013.
39. World Energy Resources. World Energy Council. 2016.

40. Yeliz Yalcin • Cengiz Arikan • Furkan Emirmahmutoglu: Determining the asymmetric effects of oil price changes on macroeconomic variables: a case study of Turkey. Springer Science+Business Media New York 2014.
41. Yi-Ming Wei • Hua Liao: Energy Economics: Energy Efficiency in China. Springer International Publishing Switzerland 2016.
42. Yukitaka Kato • Michihisa Koyama • Yasuhiro Fukushima • Takao Nakagaki: Energy Technology Roadmaps of Japan. Springer Japan 2016.
43. Yulia Veld-Merkoulova • Svetlana Viteva: Carbon Finance. Springer International Publishing Switzerland 2016.
44. Zhongfu TAN, Kangting CHEN, Liwei JU, Pingkuo LIU, Chen ZHANG: Issues and solutions of China's generation resource utilization based on sustainable development. J. Mod. Power Syst. Clean Energy. 2016.

Biography of the author

Roshdy Ebrahim Abdin, Egyptian.

Ph.D (economics)

Economics lecturer.

Member at the Egyptian assembly for political economy.

Member at the Egyptian assembly for international law.

Professional diploma in arbitration.

diploma in importing and exporting.

Lawyer since 2008.

For more information please subscribe to my blog:

http://roshdyebrahim.blogspot.com.eg/

the author's books
1. Economic study of Oil and Gas Well Drilling
2. Economic study of Oil and Gas Exploration
3. Economics of oil and gas production
4. Economics of Petroleum, principles
5. Economics of petroleum reservoirs
6. Explanatory of petroleum market volatility

www.ingramcontent.com/pod-product-compliance
Lightning Source LLC
Chambersburg PA
CBHW031617210526
45464CB00004B/1624